FIRST RULE
OF
LEADERSHIP

Achieve Far More by Leading Your Self
BEFORE You Lead Others!

DR. STEPHEN G. PAYNE

Leadership Coach and
Speaker to Top-Level
Executives Worldwide

This book is a work of non-fiction. Names of people and places have been changed to protect their privacy.

Leadership Strategies

www.LeaderX.com

ISBN: 1-4140-6012-2 (e-book)

ISBN: 1-4140-6011-4 (Paperback)

ISBN: 1-4140-6010-6 (Dust Jacket)

Library of Congress Number: 2004090214

This book is printed on acid free paper.

Printed in the United States of America

Bloomington, IN

Ist Books – rev. 2/13/04

To:

Amy and our children

*And to the clients and colleagues who shared
their extraordinary leadership journeys with me*

FIRST RULE OF LEADERSHIP

Achieve Far More by Leading Your Self
BEFORE You Lead Others!

Contents

PART ONE

The Essentials

If you're a leader and you want to be far more successful at leading, you are definitely in the right place.

Do you realize that the most valuable leadership tool you could ever possess is <u>already</u> at your disposal? Look no further than your own head. The answer to reaching the dramatically higher level of achievement you want is locked in your amazing mind. You need to unlock and activate it so that you and the rest of your team accomplish fantastic results.

*I want you to do that by constantly applying a fundamental truth of outstanding leadership. It is **The First Rule of Leadership:***

> **To lead others to success, you must first lead your self with excellence.**

You will see this rule expressed many times and in many different forms throughout this book. It is where your leadership thinking must <u>always</u> begin if you want to get the most from your leadership abilities.

I say that with certainty because I've seen how quickly careers advanced for my coaching clients who have made that choice. So please think of this book as having <u>your</u> leadership coach helping you apply The First Rule in the real world of your leadership position. You will be amazed how your results, confidence, and relationships improve when you do.

Try to remember: I'm not here to make you smarter or to give you a success formula. I'm here to help you learn a simple way to achieve far better results with the great stuff you already have.

CHAPTER ONE

Discovering The First Rule

One morning in 1994, I moved rapidly from being a successful CEO of a large international consulting business to being unemployed. I was fired. I recall vividly the awful moment when I had to explain to my wife, Amy, why I had returned from work at 10 a.m. that day.

Into the Valley

I was in a state of shock. I had always prided myself on meeting all the criteria of a "great performance." Yet there I was sinking into what I now call the Valley of Despair—pained by what had hit me and seriously questioning my leadership capabilities.

You too may have experienced a period like this. It can really give your confidence a hard knock. This one was a major career blow. It had me seriously dwelling on some of my obvious mistakes and trying to get to the real nub of my performance. What kind of leader had I, or rather hadn't I, been?

Believe me, being fired was an experience I didn't want to repeat. I felt that before tackling a new leadership position, I'd better discover the skills that made other leaders so successful, and that I clearly lacked. I decided to get myself out of the Valley by trying to discover this "secret" of leadership for myself. I picked up the phone and called as many successful leaders as I could. Then I asked them to share their leadership insights with me so I—and what turned out to be my future clients—could learn from their achievements.

As you can imagine, CEOs enjoy talking about their successes. It's a comfortably broad and open-ended topic that lets them make inspiring pronouncements. Those responses satisfy most inquirers, but not me. I hungered to understand their leadership experience at a much deeper level. I wanted to know how these men and women managed their *inner* experience—their thoughts, feelings, and reactions—as well as how they managed the outer world. Whatever the secret was, I knew that it was not some particular technique or leadership system. I'd already tried most of them. I sensed, from the shadows of my Valley, that the ability to deal with this deeper stuff was central to what I was after.

Discovering Aspects of Leadership

Immediately I noticed one major feature these leaders had in common. It was their enormous drive to make a difference. They wanted their teams to have a major impact—on their organizations and their industries. This determination was like a palpable force driving them to make a greater impact during their time at the helm. It seemed like they woke up each day with a hunger to do things better and accomplish more. I was fascinated by this drive. I wanted to know how they kept it alive, even in the dark times when *they* were in the Valley of Despair.

To be frank, I wanted some of it.

So I started asking about it. And when I did, I opened the door to a private world of leadership quite different from their public personae. We started talking passionately about the unspoken aspects of leadership: getting the *real* truth of their own performance, feeling isolated, how change impacted them, their unproductive and often chaotic team relationships (not to mention personal ones), keeping a positive attitude, balancing home and work life, and so on.

We also talked at length about the profound cascade effect these more personal things could have on their teams' performance if they didn't keep some degree of balance themselves.

I experienced a real sense of relief. I was not alone. Returning home after each meeting, I delighted in telling Amy that my own inner experiences while a CEO were similar to those felt by these great leaders.

I was starting to emerge from the Valley.

Digging Deeper to Understand Great Leadership

As I dug deeper, I began comparing the results they achieved with the inner experiences they had so candidly described. And I could see something for sure:

> *How a leader deals with what happens on his or her inner landscape is a huge predictor of what ends up happening outside.*

I could see how a lack of self-control leads to a loss of control in business, how a lack of self-respect leads to loss of respect from followers, how a compulsive need to control people ends up pushing people away. Have you noticed these things in leaders you know? Or even felt some of them in you? They are all symptoms of turmoil on a leader's inner landscape.

These successful leaders operate from a place that I never fully appreciated. Things on *their* inner landscapes—like their determination, reactions to events, and feelings of power—are much more under their management. In fact, many of them are extremely skilled at deploying parts of their inner landscapes for the good of their organizations. I'm referring to skills like focusing their attitude in support of events and people, using their positive spirit when morale is down, building clear mental images to give people straightforward pathways, and constantly transmitting how much they personally value the cooperative efforts of people in their organization.

I arrived at one company on a day when a huge financial disaster had struck. I wondered if I would find a CEO in the Valley of Despair. Not at all. She wasn't dispirited or locked away in board meetings; she was energized, organizing teams, connecting people to the truth of the situation, and sorting things out—fast. "Of course I'm disappointed, frustrated, and mad at myself for not anticipating things," she said later. "But how it feels to me is of no value to my organization and my shareholders right now."

The Leader Within

After many such interviews, I pictured another leader inside the mind of each successful leader—one the rest of us don't see directly. I pictured this *leader within* directing and governing performance from a higher vantage point, a place where he or she is managing both the inner landscape *and* the outside world. Consciously or unconsciously, this leader within is working to deploy both inner and outer resources to get the best possible performance from any situation.

I could see that when this leader within manages the inner and outer world in a well-integrated way, from what I call a *balanced platform,* the person purposefully achieves very powerful leverage from whatever leadership talents he or she has. Sometimes, particularly in stressful situations, the impact on an organization can be truly transforming. Just like that CEO in the center of a financial disaster.

Yet equally, I could see that when the leader within can not stay on a balanced platform, the downstream impact can be unproductive, even devastating. The more I questioned and looked, the more I could see how mismanagement by the leader within propagates inefficiency throughout the entire organization—even when doing something quite routine like leading a meeting, giving a speech, or providing feedback. Fortunately I also spotted how a small course correction by the leader within can transform difficult situations for the better.

I'd never fully understood this when I was a CEO. It humbled me to recognize those aspects of my own leader within that had cost me my job. I recognized how my own fear of change undermined the confidence of my team and how, when I rushed into a meeting angrily, I succeeded only in disrupting the dialogue and good work of my colleagues. I could also remember the impact of difficult relationships with colleagues on my own performance.

Now I was seeing the same effects, positive and negative, having an impact on the businesses of these CEOs.

Can you relate to these kinds of things in yourself or others? Can you recall situations where some improved management of the inner landscape could have led to far better outcomes?

Here are the nuggets about the leader within that I found in these meetings:

The very best leaders transform their organizations because they know <u>how</u> to engage the entirety of their leadership ability—their inner world as well as the outer—in each circumstance they come across.

Even when subjected to hugely disruptive unexpected events, they are able to govern themselves so that <u>all</u> their mental and emotional resources stay available for creating a great leadership performance for themselves and their team.

Less successful leaders struggle to keep their leader within on a balanced platform, particularly in high-stress situations. Some seem to ignore the platform altogether—as though a damaged autopilot is taking them inevitably to the wrong destination. As a consequence, they fail to access vital abilities they already have when they need them most. It's often quite predictable. They end up becoming a victim of circumstances rather than the master because they simply can't get their leader within functioning well.

I remember watching one red-faced manager screaming with rage at his team. He was bullying them because the program had slipped and they were not coming up with ideas to get things back on track. His team sat looking into space, some quietly fuming, some cowering, and some tuned out completely. Disaster was staring him in the face. He insisted later: "My anger is a great motivator. That's why I'm always given the people that need a good kick in the butt. They're all losers that can't do anything without me." That was the moment I saw *his* leader within quite clearly. I named it Angry Bastard.

Leaders with a malfunctioning leader within are quite common. Have you ever been on a team whose leader can't tell the truth about his or her situation? Or who insists on controlling *all* decision-making throughout the entirety of a large organization? Or who refuses to pay attention to what team members need to get their job done? Or who thinks that he is such a great speaker that he can't shut up and listen to anyone else?

These situations are nothing more than symptoms of his inability to govern his inner landscape to achieve the outcomes he needs. His leader within is not functioning for some reason. If only he could engage his leader within to work *for* him rather than against.

Total Leadership and The First Rule

Don't imagine that the great leaders I interviewed were all super-intelligent beings. Nor were they all the kind of charismatic, execution-focused dynamos the media would have us believe. They consistently deliver great results because they have the ability to manage their own mental and emotional resources to achieve the greatest outcome. They do this in the hundreds of moments that make up their day. They know they have limitations—who doesn't? But they also know that they have to constantly keep *themselves* operating from the most productive platform if their organizations are to achieve great results, irrespective of the external circumstances.

Leading this way is what I call ***Total Leadership***. It's where you fully accept and acknowledge the direct causal relationship between the results you are achieving and how your leader within governs all your inner and outer circumstances.

With Total Leadership you choose to expand your view of your accountability beyond just how well your team or organization is doing. You expand it to include being accountable for making sure your leader within is guiding *you* from the best possible platform at all times. That's why I call it "total"—you, and you alone, are leading the entire landscape, especially your inner one.

This isn't some kind of ethereal principle to remember now and again. It's something that great leaders put into practice every moment of the day. Whether they are meeting with a customer, dealing with a catastrophic event, making a speech, or giving difficult feedback, their leader within is leading the whole situation, particularly them, superbly. Simply put, to get the best results they know they must first lead themselves well.

This is the origin of ***The First Rule of Leadership***: *To lead others to success, you must first lead your self with excellence.*

(By the way, the separation between "your" and "self" in "first lead your self" is intentional. I use it throughout this book to emphasize how your leader within is leading you on your inner landscape, too.)

"The First Rule," or simply "The Rule," is what your leader within needs to understand and apply in every situation if you want to get the very best results from your leadership talent.

Let me make another point, one which I hope grabs the attention of the leader within *you*. Individuals who constantly cultivate this ability to manage themselves with The Rule, no matter what the situation, are those that achieve the rewards of being a successful leader. I say this with certainty because I've seen the level of achievement accelerate for leaders that understand this and accept full responsibility. I've even seen an Angry Bastard become a successful leader by learning to apply The Rule and turn unproductive relationships into thriving ones.

If he can do it, you can too!

Are you getting the impression that I want you to engage *your* leader within to apply The Rule? It's the single most important decision you can make if you want to improve your leadership performance permanently.

Look Honestly At <u>Your</u> Leadership

It's a fact to accept: Your leader within, like mine and everyone else's, is imperfect in its ability to guide you. But also realize that it is perfectly capable of embarking on the journey to discover and learn more.

Every leader is humbled to discover the power their leader within has to mess things up. It takes determination and courage to accept all the unsavory parts of who you are, where you've been, and the bits of your performance you really knew were complete rubbish. I should know. I've got unsavory parts sticking out all over the place. Don't you?

Also, realize that it's very easy for your leader within to be lulled into a narrow view of things. Such as one where you—or your appraisal system—convince you that you're successful when you're not (and often vice versa). Like believing you lead well because you simply got through some particular occasion. Or because your boss tells you so. Or perhaps you assume that when you do things without too much effort or without too many complaints, you are really succeeding.

The other day I heard a leader say, "Well, that went well; there weren't any problems. Nobody got upset or complained, so I'm doing great." Imagine an actor saying, "The audience turned up and applauded, so I must be a great performer." It's simply not true.

If you con yourself by keeping your view narrow enough, you can claim to be brilliant at anything—especially leadership. It's rather like saying, "Well, everyone's nodding so they must understand me." No they don't (test that one out sometime). Like a camera that's zoomed in too far, you need to zoom out, widen your aperture, and come to terms with a complete view of reality.

Here's the key point about this: *You* have the ability to be the best judge of your own performance, but only when you make the conscious choice to open up the perspective of your leader within to embrace all the inner and outer elements of your leadership work. Only when you work to make sure that you're looking at the *totality* of what impacts your leadership can you be certain that your own biases and denial tactics are not diverting you from seeing reality and therefore achieving success.

And when you are prepared to do that—to cultivate the leader within you to see the complete picture—you open yourself to the truth of leading your self:

> **When you understand the complete truth of your leadership, your leader within can guide you to a far better performance.**

Do you get that point? It's central to our work. Your future success will be a direct result of new ways to guide you, discovered by your leader within. That learning is not a process you can leave to chance, entrust to others, or base on some external system. You have to take the courageous step of accepting full accountability for your leadership by working at engaging your "whole leader" in learning how to lead you better in every kind of leadership situation.

And how do you do that? How do stop your leader within from giving up and going home? Or falling asleep on duty or denying reality? How do you wake up the leader within to stay engaged and guide you superbly toward that great leadership performance you want the world to know you for?

The question of how is what The Rule is all about. In my professional life, both as a CEO and a leadership coach, I have developed some tools and concepts that work in a wide variety of leadership situations to fully engage your leader within. They have a proven track record of being instrumental in delivering rapid improvement in performance by simply ensuring that the power of your leader within is properly engaged.

How you apply The Rule, however, is unique to you and your particular leadership journey. I wish I could simply provide you with a winning system or formula, but that just does not work. Formulas leave out the most important component—you!

I do know from experience that if your determination is strong and you actively learn to apply The Rule, you will see improved results. Results that will have a lasting impact for you, your team, and your organization. Your leader within will then be well on the way to guiding you to be the great leader you want to be.

So let's begin!

CHAPTER TWO

Learning to Apply The Rule

Your results will improve rapidly when your leader within understands the entire picture of your leadership situation and then uses this new understanding to redirect things toward a far better outcome.

From my work with many leaders, I've concluded that it's best to separate and focus on two sets of interrelated skills that correspond to how well you manage your inner and outer worlds. I call them the skills of *leading your self* and *leading others*. Look again at The Rule: *To lead others to success, you must first lead your self with excellence.* It says that, in any situation, your work is to make sure that you don't simply jump in to directing people. You first have to apply your skills of leading your self.

These skills of *leading your self* involve how your leader within harnesses the best of your own spiritual and mental potential in order to achieve more from your leadership. Because the answer to how you can reach a dramatically higher level of achievement is locked in your mind, you need to learn how to unlock it and access it in all your important leadership moments. This means working to discover new ways to overcome the obstacles that block your access to your inner potential. How can you lead your team to expanded achievement without first realizing that you—your thoughts and your reactions— are an integral part of the team's effectiveness? Remember that Angry Bastard.

The skill set of *leading others* is what people commonly refer to when they talk about leadership abilities. It is your unique way of activating your team's potential to achieve ever-greater results. The behaviors and results of the teams led by the CEOs I met reflected these abilities in ways that would be obvious to anyone. These leaders were commonly described by their teams as "visionary," "motivational," and "inspirational." Their teams' resulting achievements surpassed even their own hopes and expectations.

These two skill sets—leading your self and leading others—are very powerfully connected within every leader on all occasions. They usually operate in a seamless, automatic way. But to coach you to improved performance, I need you to take an occasional break and examine how you are leading with the skills separated. When you do, you will see far more clearly the connection between your *thinking* and the *results* you are achieving. And, if you are determined to improve things, from this new vantage point you can quickly make a required course correction.

Keep in mind that I don't just want you to read about these ideas and think they are fascinating. My challenge to you is for you to move from insight to action and, ultimately, to improve results. Therefore I want you to commit to constantly look at your leadership situation with a fresh eye and take what you learn and apply it. I urge you to rev up your determination and make that commitment right now.

Start Right Here

Think about your current leadership position and imagine yourself looking at your performance through a *lens* that has two facets. One side is showing you how well you are leading your team and your organization, the other facet is showing you how well you are leading your self on your inner landscape. As your mind reconnects the two images into your total performance, new insights start to emerge. Insights into what *you* can do to improve things for *your team.*

Here's your first look through such a lens. I'm going to pose two questions for you to answer truthfully.

1. Are you and your team achieving *all* the goals you've set and are expected of you at present? (Leading others.)

Think about the evidence of achievement you have to support your answer. It helps to make notes.

Then move on to this question about you:

2. What are *you* personally doing to make sure that your team delivers the *greatest* possible performance? (Leading your self.)

Now think about the evidence of your thinking and actions that support your answer to that second question.

Did you notice how the second question holds you accountable and pulls you personally to a higher and more valuable place from which to operate? It tugs at you to think about how to deploy your own abilities *far* more effectively—to achieve the *greatest* possible performance, not just the achievement of your goals.

Now go back and answer both questions again, but this time <u>start with the second</u>. You will feel how your answer to the first question starts to change. This is you making the connection between leading your self and leading others. Your leader within is starting to consider how to realign your leader without for a far better performance.

Repeat the process a few times and reflect on the insights that come up. You may start to change the way you are leading your team. Don't be surprised if it feels a little uncomfortable at first—your leader within is sometimes reluctant to change and take charge!

Enough questions for now. That was just an introduction. There's much more to come.

The Lens Symbol

To visually convey the way you just looked separately at how you lead your self and others, I've created this symbol to represent the lens with two facets:

Its two halves represent leadership of your inner and outer world. It implies harmony between leading your self (left side) and leading others (right side) to achieve great results.

In the center, the two halves merge into one. That's because these two halves of your leadership abilities are closely connected—in fact, they are never apart. Imagine the bars in the center as an equal sign, indicating that inner and outer leadership need to be in balance.

And yet, the left half is higher than the other. The reason why is crucial to learning to apply The Rule:

> *To lead others to success, you must FIRST lead your self with excellence.*

It says that they are both important but whenever it comes to looking at your situation, you should first think: How well am I leading my self, with my inner resources, here?

Like The Rule, you will also see the lens symbol many times throughout this book. Look upon it as a kind of mnemonic to remind you of The Rule and to prevent you from slipping back into the old habit of focusing first on what others are up to.

Looking Through a Lens at You

In this book you will use many lenses to help your leader within use The Rule to focus on your leadership. The lens is not a Magic 8 Ball, offering up specific answers. It simply provides a distinct structure for your leader within to question your performance so that insights emerge.

So, stay focused. After all, your performance in every situation is different. Your performance when managing your team, for example, looks nothing like your performance when presenting to your boss.

When you see a lens, *always* stop for a moment and let your mind go to a more peaceful state and think about the topic under consideration. That's the place I want your leader within to be standing when you look at any aspect of your performance. Fear, worry, or self-criticism won't help at all. Just have an open, ready-to-transform-things state of mind and see what happens.

This is the general layout of all the lenses you will see.

FOCUS ON A SITUATION

Leading My Self	Leading Others
Am I governing my inner world to benefit this situation — my spirit, vision, attitude, balance, determination?	Are we, as a team, performing with excellence in this situation — results, growth, alignment, relationships?

Consistent with The Rule, first ask the question about how you are leading your self (left side), and then ask the one about how you lead others (right side). Bounce back and forth a few times between the questions as we did earlier and see what insights emerge. No need to rush into action. If they're good insights they'll still be around when you put the book down.

Now here's the exercise we did earlier about achieving goals. Get into that ready-to-transform-things state of mind and try it again. Don't forget—left side first. Take a little time and answer the questions truthfully.

<u>ACHIEVING GOALS</u>

<u>Leading My Self</u>

What am <u>I</u> doing to make
sure my team delivers
the <u>greatest</u> possible
performance?

<u>Leading Others</u>

Are we, as a team,
achieving all the goals
we've set and are
expected of us?

Please don't forget that a lens always works best if you take a moment to get your leadership spirit into a positive place. Expect helpful insights to emerge. Remember that you're putting an aspect of your current leadership position under the lens so that your leader within can apply The Rule and discover insights into the forces that either promote or limit your achievement.

But also don't get so serious that you can't have a good laugh about the situation.

Humor and The Rule

I wish you could experience the laughter that goes on during face-to-face meetings when we look through lenses. There is a lighthearted, sometimes irreverent side to what happens that releases tension, pricks the over-inflated ego, and brings our raw, imperfect selves into the workspace. Nobody's perfect. And the lengths people go to avoid that reality can sometimes be hilarious.

In fact, I see humor as an essential and priceless part of growing as a leader. It's healthy to have a good laugh at the situations your leader within can get you into when you forget the simple causal relationship implied in The Rule.

You'll see some of this humor later in the book, particularly in the caricatures from the Gallery of Rogues that occasionally appear. They represent archetypically awful leaders whose leaders within consistently fail to apply The Rule. They are the bosses people love to hate and, yes, Angry Bastard is among them. I know that when a leader smiles at one of them, she is looking, in some sense, at a mirror of how her leader within can seriously mess things up. And that puts a healthy dose of reality into the conversation.

And now, it's time to get your leader within fully awake. There's an important job to be done—guiding you to a far greater performance using The Rule.

PART TWO

Awaken Your Leader Within

Your leader within can't begin to guide you to greater achievement without clear answers to some basic questions:

- *Where have I been?*

- *What good has it done me?*

- *How am I doing now?*

- *Where am I going?*

- *What do I want it to be like when I get there?*

In fact, the more you work at discovering the answers to these questions, the more confident you will become in deciding how to move forward when you apply The Rule and generate a vital insight.

In the chapters that follow, you'll be answering these questions and looking through more lenses. It's very easy to lose track of things you discover. I strongly suggest maintaining a notebook or journal for recording your responses, insights, and results. Many people find it valuable to write directly onto the pages as they are reading.

CHAPTER THREE

Your Leadership Journey

Y ou know already that I stumbled on my leadership journey. On balance, I'd prefer you not do the same.

One of the major reasons it happened was that I never realized that leadership is, just that, a "journey." It's not a series of successive life and death struggles but a steady series of events that lead toward an important destination. And, for you, that destination is the *leadership identity* you want to create by the time your journey comes to an end.

Don't be like me. Recognize that achieving the great leadership identity you want means plenty of winning and losing, succeeding and failing, valleys and mountains.

This perspective, that your leadership is a journey, is fundamental to keeping your leader within well balanced. The leader you are today can never be disconnected from the leader you were, or the leader you are becoming.

When CEOs get all puffed-up about having made it to the top, I always tell them this story.

When the former COO became the new chairman and CEO of a company, the incumbent retired and became chairman emeritus. The COO, in turn, was succeeded by the senior vice president of the company's largest manufacturing division. There was quite a retirement party; the old chairman had been with the company for 20 years and he'd seen the company through a period of substantial growth. To the investment community he was a revered industry figure.

But in his new office in the executive suite, the chairman emeritus, who always loved being in the thick of things, was growing frail. He needed a little more time to get up to speed and make his ideas understood.

The new CEO became frustrated with him. The situation peaked at the annual meeting. In making his usually uplifting speech to shareholders, the chairman emeritus stumbled occasionally and even looked hesitant about things. When some board members made comments to the CEO, he seized the moment.

"We're creating a marvelous new chairman emeritus office for you," the CEO told him the next time they met, "at the manufacturing plant on the outskirts of town. It's going to have all the high-tech trappings you need, plus it's closer to your home. It will be a much better working arrangement all around."

Shocked at the news that he was being excluded from the day-to-day operations, the chairman emeritus quietly and politely acknowledged the inevitable.

The CEO quickly delegated the planning and construction for the new office to his new COO. He asked her to rush it through. Thirty days later she came back with the design and capital approval request for the new facility at the plant.

"Wow, this is pretty expensive," said the CEO. "Why are we building *two* executive offices out at the plant?"

"Well," said the COO, "it's most cost effective if we take this opportunity to build another office out there for *you* when you retire."

Yes, *your* leadership is a journey of hard work that will pass through many phases. Make sure that your leader within accepts that fact completely. The price of winning can never be the journey itself—for you or your team. Try not to let the rewards of any position be your exclusive focus. When you keep your leader within in the "journey state of mind," you learn to value the growth opportunity offered by each moment.

Frankly, on many occasions, simply continuing to engage the best of yourself on your journey will be all the reward you'll ever get.

It's All One Great Journey

Think of yourself as on a journey that touches and shapes the experiences of others, especially those that follow you.

As you grow as a leader, you are growing in the way you help your followers find meaning, success, and joy on their own journeys. So the growth of your organization, the growth of your team members, and your own growth are all part of *one* great journey. Whether you are a parent, a soldier, a pastor, the leader of your country, or the CEO of a global corporation, you are constantly called upon to embody great leadership and inspire it in others—wherever your journey takes you.

Don't confuse this with the leaders described by the static models you learn about in most books, seminars, or case studies. They can certainly illustrate leadership insights for all people and sometimes for all time. But they don't speak to *you*—your particular personality, experience, and set of circumstances. The one great leadership journey of interest here is yours and yours alone.

A Journey of Unique Moments

The term "moments" has specific meaning here. Memory doesn't come in neat packages—in stories with a beginning, middle, and end. It comes through visual, experiential moments. So does life on your journey. The ones we're going to concentrate on are "leadership moments"—those times in your life when you create impact as a leader. You experience the charge of such moments differently each time. You might feel successful in one—optimistic, happy, and growing. In another, you could be feeling confused and have no clue where you're headed. Most moments actually have both positive and negative charges.

These leadership moments happen all the time: when you speak before a group, meet someone for the first time, solve a problem, run a meeting, or interview a potential member of your team. Sometimes even when you simply pick up the phone. The other day, I was slaving over a computer spreadsheet, focusing on numbers, sums, cells, and arrays, when a colleague called. "Hi! How are you?" she said. "What do you want?" I barked without thinking. Then I caught myself. In that moment, I wasn't focused on her and I certainly wasn't focused on leading. I first had to clear my head of the nitpicking details of my other task.

This is what a leadership journey is really like every day. It's not so much about models and theory. It's about the real world of your job and the work you need to get done today. And how you're thinking, feeling, and acting as you're doing it.

Leadership Moments

The times on your leadership journey when you have the opportunity to maximize your impact as a leader. There are thousands of leadership moments on your journey.

It's *you, the leader,* in real time. And that's exactly where you put The Rule into action—in each and every leadership moment. Not simply in the fuzzy, idealized future, but in the complicated, messy reality of where you are today and what you have to achieve. You don't get to pick and choose moments. The First Rule is for them all, no matter what they contain:

To lead others to success you must first, in each leadership moment, lead your self with excellence.

Of course, you've been on this journey for some time, whether you were fully aware of it or not. Take time to look back and see how you've grown and changed. Can you envision that same growth in the future? Are you ready to commit to more growth? To realize that barriers and problems along the way are gateways to new possibilities? To believe that the journeys of your followers are as important as achieving the results you expect?

Time Out for a Question!

Wait a minute, here. Please don't speed past those questions without a thought. They aren't merely rhetorical. The success of your journey depends a great deal on how you ask and answer questions about yourself and your performance.

Your own good sense can offer you much more guidance than you may imagine. If you get your leader within to ask the right questions, in each leadership moment, the answers will yield insights that will improve your future performance. That's how more success comes quickly—not from role-playing, attending a seminar, or conforming to the views of others, but from putting in the mental effort to see your own performance *as you lead*. You will also be amazed at how much more confidence you feel when you learn how to ask and answer the *right* questions for yourself.

So once in a while, as you're reading, you'll come across a box like the one that follows. Its purpose is to slow the pace and allow your leader within to reflect on a topic. Before you begin answering the questions in a box, take a moment to put yourself in a reflective state of mind. Read it over once or twice to familiarize yourself with the content. Then bring your mind to rest, concentrating on the first question. Let whatever images or ideas arise enter your mind freely. Be patient. There are no deadlines, so do answer all the questions, and do so honestly.

This is a good time to give you a final reminder that many successful leaders find it invaluable to keep a journal. Answering these questions is an excellent way to use one. In fact, writing down the answers that emerge is an excellent exercise in itself. The act of writing inspires new thoughts and leads to connections and consequences that might not develop otherwise. But no matter how you approach these exercises, the important thing is to learn to make space in your life for reflection about yourself. It's essential to applying The Rule.

Now try the questions.

Leadership Moments on Your Journey

Pause now and reflect on these questions about your leadership journey thus far.

1. *Picture two or three people whose lives were shaped by your leadership (in either positive or negative ways). Recall the leadership moments when you had an impact on each of them. These moments don't have to be dramatic.*

2. *Remember times when you were called upon to be a leader. How did you respond? Were there occasions when you accepted willingly? Others when you hesitated or lacked enthusiasm? Did this initial attitude affect the outcome of each situation?*

3. *Can you remember leadership moments when you failed miserably to achieve your purpose? Was there a disaster, or did it just feel like there was? Replay those moments in your mind, and imagine them the way you would have preferred them to go.*

4. *What are the top five successes in your career so far? What tangible pieces of evidence do you have on your "Trophy Shelf" to say that you are already a successful leader?*

Conclude this exercise by looking ahead to your next three important leadership moments in the next few days. What do you need to do to make these "Trophy Shelf" moments?

Question 4 in the box—about evidence of your leadership success on your **Trophy Shelf**—is my challenge to you for the moment. Take a look at that question again. The point is not merely to have pleasant thoughts of your past, but to document solid evidence of success in your life. Use it to let your leader within recall that you *already are* a successful leader. You have proof—like promotions, articles you've authored, awards, a nice lifestyle, and such.

Results too quickly forgotten—and evidence too quickly put aside— may show that your leader within is on a day trip instead of a true leadership journey. I know firsthand that day trips are fun, but don't be seduced into mistaking them for steps toward the true destination of your leader within.

What about those negative leadership moments? What if you failed to reach a certain goal? What about mistakes? Think about this: Have you ever noticed that serious failure never seems to occur as the result of a single mistake by a leader? It's true. Most major failures in leadership are the result of *repetitive* mistakes—often mistakes of the most basic kind. These patterns can send your career into a downward spiral.

The trick, then, isn't avoiding mistakes. (You can't, unless you hide under your desk.) The trick is to avoid *repeating* mistakes. Of course, that's not as easy as it sounds. In fact, helping with that task is a central part of my coaching.

> *By discovering the thought and behavior patterns in how you lead your self, you can root out the causes of repetitive mistakes and play out your leadership moments in new ways.*

Think again about question 2 in the box—about your attitude upon accepting new leadership roles. Do you find a relationship between your attitude at the onset of a task and the outcome of that task? Very often, a poor attitude leads to poor results, while a strong attitude leads to success. Remember that Angry Bastard in the first chapter. That's no coincidence! The Rule implies there is a direct, causal relationship between your core attitude and the results you achieve through the people you lead.

Here's another lens. In this case, I want you to focus on the next important leadership moment you will face in your job. Perhaps you will be leading a meeting, interviewing someone, or giving directions for a new task. (Remember: Start with the question on the left, then go right, then ask the same questions a few more times bouncing back and forth.)

NEXT MOMENT

Leading My Self

Leading Others

How will I manage my presence to raise the level of accomplishment beyond the norm?

Are we all clear what level of accomplishment and quality is expected of us?

This lens demonstrates the power of The Rule in planning your activities. Can you feel how the lens pushes you to be more conscious of your attitude and your behavior so that, *before* your next important moment, you do your best to raise accomplishment for the team? Not by becoming overly self-conscious, but by targeting *your* contribution to be far better. And when you do that, you set the example for your team to do the same.

There will be millions of these leadership moments on your journey. Don't make the mistake of winging it or expecting them all to be perfect. If you learn to use the lens and to consciously apply The Rule, these moments will create a new path—to the successful leadership identity you dream of achieving.

CHAPTER FOUR

People That Influence You

$\mathbf{I}$t's amazing how much we are influenced by others on our journey. I'm reminded of a great comedy sketch in *Monty Python's Flying Circus* in which a family at home discovers they've got, of all things, a dead bishop in the house. After hilarious happenings, it transpires that the father is the "one wot done it."

As he is arrested, he declares loudly, "It was <u>society</u> that made me do it!"

"Well," says the police officer, "we'll be arresting them as well."

No, society is not to blame for the leader you have become. But your leader within *is* strongly influenced by many people in society.

We all tend to emulate those we love and admire. We borrow their catchphrases and adopt their style. Then we take these things into our key leadership moments and try to be leaders like them. Likewise, we tend to subconsciously take on the traits of people around us—even when they're not so flattering.

So honing this circle of influencers around you is essential to every stage of your leadership journey. If you let your leader within be influenced by fools, what kind of influencer will you be to your team?

Your Personal Board of Directors

Look back over the successes in your life. Were there times when you seemed to grow rapidly (particularly in new jobs) and other times when things slowed down? During such times of high growth, were there leaders who influenced you substantially? My bet is that the answer is yes and that you probably even meet with some of them in person from time to time to tap into their wisdom.

There are other strong influencers too, like family members, former bosses, and teachers. They might even be historical leaders you have studied. Whether aware of it or not, you probably try to emulate them at times. (I'm a Winston Churchill fan. He's influenced me so much that without too much prompting I'll get to my feet and do my impersonation of his speeches.) These influential leaders are with you in a very real way influencing the way you lead today. Just ask members of your team!

Start picturing this group of influential leaders as your personal ***Board of Directors.*** They have a powerful governance role in the way your leader within is directing your journey. Some you learn from directly through conversation and observation. Others you simply admire and try to emulate.

Board of Directors

Influential leaders who have a strong governance role in all your leadership moments.

It's important that you recognize the value each Board member brings (or fails to bring) you on your leadership journey. You may owe some of your strengths to these people. You may also have discovered that being influenced by the wrong people can put you on the wrong track. Like any organization, you need a Board that is experienced, ethical, unbiased, truthful, and supportive.

Keep Your Board Active

Your personal Board should be a dynamic entity. If too many members are distant figures from history or public life, recruit some people nearby who are willing to help you in person. Rigorously examine the contribution each person brings. If it's deficient, be prepared to give that person a mental backseat and elect—or promote—someone more appropriate. Fire some Board members, if necessary.

Think now about who influences you in your current leadership job and look into the next lens. (Remember the lens routine: get calm, left side first, etc., and be truthful.)

BOARD OF DIRECTORS

Leading My Self

Are all the people who influence my leadership properly qualified, ethical, truthful, and supportive?

Leading Others

Am I exposing my team to people who exhibit the leadership capabilities and performance we need?

One of the reasons I lost my CEO job was that I let my leader within be overly influenced by my previous bosses. With them I'd experienced and emulated the wrong way to respond to certain situations. There were serious repercussions when those same situations occurred when I was in charge.

Through my coaching, I've discovered that this problem is very common indeed. Many times, the simple step of getting your leader within to replace an offending and overly influential Board member can have an enormous impact on accelerating performance.

Don't forget that all active members of your Board grow along with you on their own journey. In helping you develop, they grow themselves—not just through the results you achieve, but through insights they discover about themselves. This kind of relationship is invaluable to you in understanding your leadership abilities, particularly when stretching into a new role or if you are in the early stages of your leadership journey.

But no matter what the stage of your journey, never forget this: *You are a candidate for the Board of Directors of every single person you will ever lead.*

Create a Dynamic Board of Directors

1. Recall 10 leaders who have had a great influence over the way you <u>now</u> lead. Think in terms of family, community, work, and leaders of whom you've read.

2. Picture experiences that accelerated your leadership growth. Were they enhanced by the presence of a strong leader? Have any leaders <u>decelerated</u> your journey?

3. Create a list of your current personal Board of Directors members, including people you treat as mentors and advisers. Rate them each according to their degree of influence over you, <u>and</u> the real value of their advice.

4. Think about your leadership job and the near-term success expected of you. Are there gaps in your Board? Do you need to recruit (or fire) members in order to exceed that expectation?

Finish this exercise by setting up an action plan for recruiting and meeting with new Board members.

CHAPTER FIVE

Master Your Strengths

There's something almost all of us fired CEOs say: "At some deeper level, I could see it coming but I didn't know how to get out of the way." It's the feeling of being downstream of a giant wave we started but can't stop. Or like we loaded a faulty program into the autopilot and no matter how hard we work, the wrong destination just keeps getting closer and closer.

In my case, my autopilot was damaged by my belief that everything required my attention. In the months before I got fired I was working 80 hours per week, running businesses on three continents, plus thinking that I could single-handedly manage a huge crisis with our largest customer. This, according to my autopilot, was how to be a successful leader. I spent little time with my executive teams. It was not a pretty sight. The giant wave was coming and I couldn't stop.

Here's the nugget:

> *You're not, and never will be, brilliant at everything. You're not even good at lots of things, but be really clear about what you are good at and cultivate it.*

Your first task, then, is to truly know what you're good at. The second is to understand whether it constitutes a leadership strength worth cultivating.

Get Clear About Your Strengths

Creating an inventory of your leadership strengths should be easy, right? Just pull out the latest copy of your performance evaluation or 360° feedback and fill in the blanks.

Not quite. While there are many feedback systems and performance-management tools that seek to describe your leadership strengths in different ways, be cautious; these instruments are all very helpful, but don't regard them as the absolute truth about you. Their purpose is to evaluate you and make suggestions based on a model of strengths defined by *someone else*—someone who is not on your unique leadership journey, and, most likely, is not among the people you trust on your personal Board of Directors.

In the most basic sense, your leadership strengths are your *personal* strengths. They include both your inherent gifts (the things that you are naturally good at) and acquired abilities—those skills, attitudes, competencies, and approaches to problem-solving that you know really work for you (for example: public speaking and conflict resolution). They're strengths because you've successfully demonstrated them time and again. They produce great results for you. Also included on this list would be experience in and knowledge of a particular field, as well as the values and beliefs you hold dear and bring to every role you perform.

Surprisingly, talent doesn't always translate into strength. Even the best leaders have the unfortunate knack of making a strength into weakness. Do you know a great presenter who won't listen to you and your team, or a great controller who can't leave people to manage on their own? Do you remember how that Angry Bastard thought his anger was his greatest strength and a great motivator of his team? Later you'll meet some of his awful colleagues in the Gallery of Rogues, like Judge Mental, Micromanager Mary, and the Slick Prince. Why do they believe they have great strengths yet the results produced by their leadership can be so terrible?

Here's the next nugget:

> *A strength is not just about you. It's about your team and their performance as a result of you.*

Be careful here. This point is fundamental and often overlooked. Make sure your leader within equates strength with the results it delivers consistently for your team. As I discovered to my detriment, a solo performance, admirable as it may be, is no strength unless it motivates your team to a greater performance.

If you can't see the connection between your view of your strengths and your team's performance, ask each team member this: What is it that I do that consistently helps you achieve a great performance? Then *listen*! Next, ask them what you do that consistently does the opposite. Then *listen* again.

Here's another lens. Think about that definition of strength: It's not just about you, it's about your team and their performance as a result of you. Then focus on your current leadership situation and look through the lens with the usual left-then-right routine.

```
                    PLAY FROM STRENGTH

      Leading My Self              Leading Others

      Am I deploying my           Are my team members
   strengths to enable great    demonstrating that I have
      performances and          them in roles that play
   empowering others to         from their strengths?
   compensate for my
       weakness?
```

It's easy to let denial blur your vision when looking through this lens. So I urge you to enlist the help of one or two active members of your Board and ask them to look through the lens with you. Share your definition of your strengths with them so they can keep you honest. I want you to get your leader within *completely* certain about them. They are the solid foundation of your expanding leadership platform.

Stretch and Grow From Strength

People often say that leadership is a gift that cannot be learned. That is only half true. We all have roughly the same leadership components, just as we all have the same set of muscles in our bodies. But each of us, through years of use, have developed some gifts much more than others. In fact, those gifts, whether learned or innate, continue to develop all the time if you work at them. They grow the same way our muscles grow when we train them—whenever we stretch ourselves into new roles and responsibilities.

As with physical challenges, these stretch periods are never entirely comfortable, but they are an essential element of growth. When you think about your Board of Directors, you probably recall a lot of stretch periods when a member of your Board was there to help and encourage you. That's not surprising. Good stretch periods can be the most rewarding and memorable parts of your career.

> *You can't expect to grow as a leader unless you are willing to stretch.*

But stretch from your strong muscles not your weak ones. Sometimes it seems like the very best you've got from your upbringing, experience, knowledge, and beliefs—not to mention your intelligence and sparkling personality—are never enough. Are they really all you have to bring to each moment on your leadership journey? Yes! What's more, they're all you need. Fortunately for all of us, super-intelligence is not a prerequisite for great leadership. Just get your leader within clear about your strengths and how they enable a great team performance and you won't have difficulty stretching and keeping balanced.

Before you list your strengths, don't forget this key point: Your team is observing you and your strengths as though you're under a microscope. That's because each of them has a leader within that's tapping into those parts of your strengths that enable them to be successful. This is how your strong muscles do real leadership work for the entire team. When you don't apply The Rule and you become preoccupied with ameliorating weakness, your weak muscles can do no more than engender a weak team performance.

So be confident of your strengths. That feeling of being dissected by your team is to be expected and welcome. You want your team to see how to use their strong muscles to compensate for your weak ones. That's how you build a strong organization, one full of leaders.

Be Clear on Your Core Strengths

List only strengths that are evidenced by your history of leadership performance and/or affirmed by your Board of Directors.

1. *What are the strengths* you will always bring to any leadership role you commit to? Be broad and generous with yourself but make sure you have seen the results of these strengths reflected in the performance of your team.*

2. *Now, take real pride in yourself and recall one thing you have always been good at doing that helps other people on their journey. All you have to do is complete this phrase: "People have always told me how much they enjoyed the way I help them succeed when I _____."*

When you have completed this exercise, write the strengths down and keep the list where you can read it every week. Acknowledge them often. Be very grateful for them.

* Suggestion: Some leaders tend to describe their strengths in terms of <u>skills</u>, like public speaking or problem-solving. Others tend to describe strengths in terms of their <u>knowledge and experience</u>, like technical know-how or track record. Still others see their strengths in terms of <u>deeply-valued elements of themselves</u>, like their drive and friendliness or their belief and commitment to a cause. Use all three definitions and see if you can come up with two core strengths in each category—six strengths in total. Remember, they must equate to results delivered consistently with your team or be confirmed as such by your Board.

Take a Look in the Mirror

When you thought about your successful leadership moments, your personal Board of Directors, and your strengths, did you start labeling yourself as good or bad? Did you start complaining that you have too few strengths or tell yourself that you've picked the wrong Board, or did you decide that you had too little success thus far on your journey?

Don't be such a Judge Mental! It prevents you from maintaining balance between how you lead your self and how you lead others. Or worse, your harsh self-judgment fans the flames of your anxiety and passes them on to your team. You are who you are, and you've been where you've been, and you've got the wonderful strengths you've got. What matters far more is where you are going and how your leader within will take you to an even better performance by learning The Rule.

I mentioned earlier the more lighthearted (yet still very important) part of Total Leadership. Let me start introducing my Gallery of Rogues: a group of horribly out-of-balance leaders you will love to hate. You'll find members of the Gallery throughout the book. Please note that although the caricatures are depicted as either women or men, they are all gender neutral.

Each Rogue is a caricature, a tongue-in-cheek expression of a leader in the mind of a follower—*not*, it's important to mention, in the mind of the leader. You see these characters in organizations every day, plus all the chaos they create. You might even recognize yourself in one or two. You'll see the way their leader within thinks as well as what they say to others when they fail to apply The Rule. Look at how the out-of-balance thinking manifests itself to others.

All the Rogues appear in a mirror frame. That's because I want you to look closely and see if you recognize some of that Rogue in you. It's another way of awakening your leader within.

Most leaders discover that a few of these Rogues resonate with them quite loudly. Take time to study each one and understand the underlying message about how you lead your self. If it speaks to you, take heed of what it says under "Is this you?"

JUDGE MENTAL

Judge to Self

I know the best way.

I'm right, they're wrong.

I'm not succeeding enough!

Judge to Others

"Let's do it right this time."

"That's the stupidest thing I've ever heard."

"You've got a long way to go."

Is this you?

Leadership is not a vehicle for you to impose your will. Listen.

Positive Strength

Decisive.

CHAPTER SIX

Make a *Big* Difference

Here's a quick mental exercise to gauge your impact. There are two parts.

First, imagine what you and your team are hoping to achieve for your organization over the next couple of years (or time periods). Take a second to think about it. What are the things you want to achieve over the next two years?

Next, imagine the same thing without you present—as though you left or stopped working for your organization today. What would be achieved over two years *without* you?

Now what's the difference between those two pictures?

The difference is you, of course—what you imagine will be created as a result of your leadership.

Your Leadership Identity

Think of this difference as your mental picture of what you want your leadership to achieve. Large or small, it's what you imagine the downstream impact of all your leadership moments will look and feel like when you "get there."

I call it your ***leadership identity***. It's a private space in your mind containing the hopes, dreams, and results you *truly* want your leadership to create. Part real, part fantasy, it's a very powerful image of who your leader within wants to become.

Now repeat the exercise with this as the first question: If you knew you *couldn't fail*, what would you like to achieve over the next two years? Write that one down. It's a measure of just how high you're willing to set the bar.

If you let it, this leadership identity in your mind can have incredible power. It's the image of the leader you want to become that draws you forward. Not just the results you want to achieve but also what you imagine and hope all the trappings of success will feel like when you get there. The more you work with it, enjoy it, and give it clarity, the more determined you'll feel that you really will become that person.

Leadership Identity

The greatest impact you want your leadership to have on the world. The footprint you want your leadership to leave behind.

When I look back, I realize how closely I watched the previous CEOs of the last company I worked for. I wanted to become one of the leaders. And so I often visualized what I could do for the organization, given the chance. My determination grew strong. Every time these people failed at something I saw the path I would take given half the chance. And when the chance came I took it and tried to achieve a greater vision of the business. Although I got fired, I never regret traveling the road of trying to bring my leadership identity to life—warts and all. On the contrary, losing my job eventually enabled me to craft a new leadership identity—the one you're experiencing in this book. I'm becoming a better leadership coach—much wiser about my warts, too.

Does your leader within do this kind of thinking about your future? It's important leadership work. When I hear my clients express their determination to beat their competition or run a larger company or get to the next level in their organization, I know they're doing the important work of maintaining a leadership identity that's much greater than the one they have. They're doing serious thinking that builds the concrete images that give clarity to their real purpose. It's The Rule in action: *To lead others to a better place, first get your self clear about the better place you're trying to get to.*

You may have read about these ideas in autobiographies. Famous leaders often look back and realize that they knew with complete certainty what they had to achieve. It felt like their inner spirit and their leadership identity were so clear and well aligned that they just knew they couldn't fail. In their darkest moments, this belief was all they had to get through. Not that they didn't make mistakes—who doesn't—but in their mind's eye their determination to achieve their leadership identity was unassailable.

There's a more down-to-earth way to say this. If you're not clear where you're headed, where do you expect your team is going?

Determination to Build Your Identity

How strong is your determination to make a difference? Is it a spark or a flame? Is it unassailable? Or is the footprint you want to make on the world looking a bit wishy-washy and soggy?

DETERMINATION

Leading My Self

Am I determined to build a great leadership identity in my job? Do I know how to <u>stay</u> determined?

Leading Others

Is my determination enabling my team to sustain their focus on achieving success?

We're talking about your determination to make a positive and successful difference as a leader. This is far more than the determination to just take a shower and show up. It's the determination to engage the best of who you are to make things better in every one of your leadership moments.

I can guarantee that your leadership identity will come under attack from people and events throughout your entire journey. So without this kind of determination you're sunk. It's the *driving* force behind your leader within. And without it, lots of it, the leadership identity you create has no meaning.

> *Without determination to keep building your greater identity, your leadership journey ends up on someone else's path.*

To keep your determination strong, you need to be clear as to what's driving you. I mean the things you want or don't want that get you in motion. Is it money? Power? Helping people? If you don't stay clear on what drives you, you can lose your determination. And then you can't be bothered to keep a strong leadership identity. Eventually you and your team put in a poor performance.

Start fanning the flames of your urge for a greater leadership identity today. This private image of your future is not something that should pop into your mind when your job security feels threatened. Nor is it something you should expect others to create for you or something you suppress whenever you encounter a disappointment. It's a crucial part of the work your leader within needs to do.

It comes down to this: Do you want your team to make a big difference or don't you?

If you do, your leader within also needs to accept this fundamental point:

> *You must do the thinking work of building your greater leadership identity and then use its power, in every leadership moment, to bring it to fruition.*

If you're clear on where you are trying to get to and how you want it to be when you get there, you are far better equipped to judge each step along the way.

Keeping a Clear Leadership Identity

What if you could see *all* the possibilities that rise before you? Would you be willing to think even bigger, reach even higher? Think seriously about what "making a big difference" means to you. Perhaps you want public acknowledgment, additional responsibilities, raises, or management recognition for your contribution. Consider all your options. Maybe you and your team are trying to make a real impact on people and results. What if there were unlimited possibilities for you? What really caused you to pick up this book in the first place?

It's this kind of questioning that jolts your leadership identity into life sometimes. But it should never be a once-in-a-blue-moon event.

> *Constantly creating and deploying a clear leadership identity for your self is a strength worth its weight in gold.*

It's a strength that can bring about truly exceptional results for you and your team. Leaders that disregard or overlook this are those that easily lose their resolve and head down the pathway to mediocrity. They end up frustrated with others when they don't see enough progress toward the team's goals. They're also the first to say their career isn't moving as fast as they would like.

If you too have these reactions to roadblocks, start recognizing that they're symptoms that your leadership identity lacks the force to draw you *beyond* the obstacles. You're not doing the private thinking work of creating a clear image of where you want to get to and how you want it to feel. Next time you blame your boss or your circumstances for your lack of progress, ask yourself instead why your leadership identity isn't sufficiently vivid and exciting to enable your leader within to propel you to radically change your situation for the better. Or ask what keeps killing your determination to change.

Don't let any discomfort you feel turn you away from this. That feeling of not being able to achieve all you want can actually be your friend. It's a positive force that triggers you to do the planning work you need. It pushes you to take responsibility for your journey and give your leadership identity more meaning.

This is not just a vague, high-minded idea about your goals in life. It's the pragmatic truth of every leadership moment that you will experience today. Apply The Rule: Start by being clear on the impact *you* want in each moment. When you are clear in those moments, your obstacles will likely be far more obvious, as well. You can't conquer what you can't see.

Finally, recognize that your leadership identity is *completely* under your management. It exists entirely in your mind. When you fully accept this point and get your leadership identity working for you, you will know what empowerment can really feel like.

Building Your Leadership Identity

The purpose of this exercise is to reflect on who and what drives you to achieve your desired leadership identity:

1. *What are you and your team hoping to achieve for your organization in the next year or so? Who and what is driving you to do that?*

2. *Imagine what achievement would look like if you said one year from now, "Wow, I've amazed myself!" Whose drive and determination do you need to change right now for you to get there?*

3. *List the kinds of people and situations that (a) help you build and sustain a leadership identity that motivates you, and (b) destroy your determination and undermine your leadership identity.*

Ask yourself: Am I willing to choose to do more of 3(a) and a lot less of 3(b) and raise the bar for my team? What's stopping you?

The Amazing Story of Howard and His Fish

Howard Coward's leadership identity was lacking because he was so ruled by fear. When he pictured his future leadership impact, his vision was fogged by his terror of any situation that could go wrong or lead to confrontation. I bet you know people just like him.

He was ambitious but never a top performer. He left his position as regional division manager to join another company as vice president at its corporate offices. In the first week of his new position, as he was settling in, he got a call from the chairman's office asking him to come by.

"Howard, welcome to the company," said the chairman, who was rushing out. "We're having a leadership team retreat this weekend at my favorite fishing lodge, and I want to make sure that you come. Can you? The group will be just over 100. It includes spouses and significant others, plus some of our competitors and their spouses."

"Err...yes sir," said Howard.

"Great," said the chairman, "See you Friday evening at the lodge. Gotta go."

Howard hurried back to his office and called his wife, telling her to cancel the plans they'd already made. He'd been hoping for a restful two days, but now, anxious about interacting with his new boss and colleagues, Howard dreaded the weekend.

On Friday evening, Howard and his wife arrived late at the lodge, and as they were checking in, the chairman emerged from the bar to greet them. "I was hoping to see you a little earlier, Howard," he said. "I wonder if I could ask you to make the welcome speech tomorrow. It's a great chance for everyone to get to know you. Introduce yourself and your wife, introduce my wife and me, and welcome the team and the competitors and their spouses. You know—that sort of thing. Also, as the new guy on the block, we'd like you to give us your views on company strategy and goals. We want to hear what you think of our direction, what you find so great about it, and why you chose to join us. Inspire us all, Howard. Of course, don't give the competitors too much! We start at 8:30 a.m. See you then."

HOWARD COWARD

Howard to Self

I'm scared of what
can happen to me.

Never volunteer!

Don't make any
mistakes!

Howard to Others

"Err, I was
wondering if ..."

"I hate to ask you
this, but .."

"We'll do it when
we have to."

Is this you?

Be clear about what _you_ want to gain
in a situation rather than
fearing what you might lose.

Positive Strength

Assessing
risk/benefit.

"Err…okay," said Howard, entrails liquefying as his boss walked back to the bar.

Howard kissed his wife good night and got out his trusty laptop. He was still sitting there at 2 a.m., imagining every possible disaster that could befall his presentation, when sleep got the better of him. He was awake with worry at 6 and started working on his presentation again.

At some point, the thought occurred to him that he could always get another job. By 8 he was dressed and heading to the hall with his laptop, nearly paralyzed with fear. When the chairman's assistant told him there was no projector available, panic set in.

He chose to avoid reality. He walked out of the lodge to the lake and as he looked across it, the terrible thought occurred to him to dive in and swim until he sank.

Surely not that, thought Howard, and turned from the lake, almost in tears. Just then, he noticed some fishing rods leaning against a tree. Why not? he thought. He baited a hook and started casting idly, though he could barely concentrate on what he was doing.

You should hear the rest of this story as Howard told it to me.

"I was never so scared in my life. There I was, about to make an enormous fool of myself in front of the chairman, my wife, my boss, my colleagues, and our competitors—everyone. I was in deep s---. At best, what I had to offer was flimsy. I was trying to think of how to avoid embarrassing myself with the competitors so I could get a job with them after I was fired. I remember vaguely hearing my wife's voice in the distance, telling me that it was 8:25 and time to go in. I ignored her completely.

"Then I got this huge bite. You won't believe this, but I got an enormous salmon on my line that was thrashing about in front of me. I couldn't cut the line, so I had to try to land it. My wife was loudly insisting I come in when I finally got it close to the shore and landed it.

"It was a monster—at least three feet long—the biggest fish I ever caught. I couldn't believe I'd done it. My fear turned to pride. I thought, not bad, Howard! So I put the rod down and picked up the fish in my arms and walked back into the lodge where my wife was looking really worried because people were already seated and waiting. Well, I just knew what I had to do. I just kept walking. I burst through the doors of the hall with the fish in my arms, and everybody turned and looked. I stood for a second until there was quiet, then I walked to the front of the stage and said into the microphone, "Good morning, everyone, and welcome. I'm Howard. I just caught *my* fish for the weekend—I hope yours will be twice as big."

"The place erupted. I felt 10 feet tall. I didn't give my presentation; I just gave a big welcome to everyone and told them that the fish said it all for me—what a great catch I had made in joining the team and all that. I even forgot to introduce the chairman and the spouses, but it was a fantastic weekend for my wife and me. People just kept coming over and mentioning my fish and saying how great it was.

"The next week, the head of human resources came over to my office and told me the chairman put me on his list of high-potential fast-track leaders."

Now put yourself in Howard's shoes. What happened at that lake? With that fish, he was not afraid to speak. He was proud, courageous, and determined.

The fish symbolizes what exists in every leader. From the private lake of his wishy-washy leadership identity, he pulled out something that was solid gold and a delight to see. He found something that was clear, tangible, relevant, exciting, and even entertaining. He was confident, balanced, and inspiring. His impact was authentic and memorable. He found a core of his leadership identity that he was proud of, one he was determined to show fearlessly. Nothing could sway his confidence—not making mistakes, not being unprepared, nothing. People instantly accepted him, because they could see how empowered he was by his fish.

His *Fish* (now capitalized and a Total Leadership word used throughout this book) was Howard's bold statement: "This is what I stand for as a leader. This is the core of my leadership identity you can always count on being there. I am determined to succeed wherever I take it."

How's your Fish today? Does it deliver the kind of message to people that Howard's did? Is the core of your leadership identity as *tangible* as Howard's? Are you prepared to hold it boldly in front of you so that your determination is clear to everyone? Or are you still at the wishy-washy lake casting to find the essence of who you are?

Leadership Fish

The short, powerful statement of the core of your leadership identity—who you are and what you always stand for.

From working with many Fishes, I've learned that if you can describe your Fish succinctly, say in 25 words or less, then it gains far more potency. It becomes something you can remember and recall when your leader identity is buffeted by the rough waves at Lake Wishy-washy.

Try it. And when you've got it, start telling your team, your colleagues, and your boss about it. You will be amazed how people respond to your leadership when you are clear and strong about what you stand for.

CHAPTER SEVEN

Be Clear About Your Purpose

When you work at expressing your purpose in concrete terms, you start to bring your leadership identity to life. Simply put, it's far easier to move toward a clear object than a fuzzy one. But what should your purpose be?

Have you ever watched leaders operate when their purpose is not clear—or worse, when their stated purpose and real purpose are obviously at odds? What a disaster! I recently observed a CEO who was two years from retirement. She kept saying that her organization's purpose was to invest and grow for the long term. Yet she constantly made decisions that cut developmental activity in favor of profits. People started leaving the company in search of better growth opportunities. After she retired, the firm took a major dive. I discovered later that her pension was tied to the profits of the company in her last two years as CEO. What was her real purpose—growth or a good pension?

Another one I just heard about (you may have, too): A company that recently went into bankruptcy had been encouraging its employees to buy stock right up to the moment of collapse. But the executive team sold theirs and paid themselves fat early bonuses before the business tanked. No need to ask what their purpose was.

Defining Your Leadership Purpose

Let me suggest a definition of purpose that will guide your leader within in every leadership moment:

> *The purpose of your leadership is to <u>improve outcomes</u>—for your organization, for your team, for those individuals who depend upon your organization, and for yourself.*

So if you are not consistently *improving outcomes* (or *results*), you are not yet achieving your purpose as a leader. By contrast, if you *are* achieving outcomes despite a perceived weakness (I'm not political! Confrontation terrifies me! I need to create more consensus!), that "weakness" really isn't as important as you thought. Think about that the next time you complete your self-evaluation or read your 360° feedback report.

Take the time to ponder this definition of purpose, particularly the last two words. Is it selfish or in some way distasteful to want to improve outcomes for yourself? Read the whole definition again and recognize that *your* outcomes are among many. Nevertheless, they are there. Remember The Rule—that you must first lead your self. How can you lead your self if *you* do not benefit in some measurable way from the outcome? Aren't your achievements a powerful part of your leadership identity?

Keep Your Focus on Outcomes

Expressing your purpose in terms of outcomes warrants a word of caution. Unfortunately, the outcomes worth pursuing are seldom as clear as we would wish. In fact, they can be very vague indeed.

Leadership Outcomes

Tangible, observable results, accomplished under your leadership, that benefit your organization, those that depend upon your organization, and you.

One major reason is that such ideal outcomes are often masked by the norms of the culture in which you work. For example, there is often a major difference between the public and private language we use to express our wants and needs.

Put simply:

> ***The outcomes you say you want and what you really want are often not the same.***

Like asking for your boss's job—you have to find the culturally acceptable code for expressing the outcomes you want.

Keep in mind that success is not just a feeling. It's the tangible, observable consequence of your efforts and those of your team. And by extension, outcomes aren't mere ideals. They are concrete results that your leadership delivers at precise times. So success is largely a *series* of improving measurable outcomes.

Feelings can be very misleading when it comes to considering your success. You may feel good about your leadership and the general state of your team, but that is *not* achieving your purpose. When your leadership effort consistently produces the tangible results you want and that are expected of you—no matter how short-term they may be—you are truly achieving your leadership purpose. And *that's* worth feeling good about.

But when people on your team say they feel good even though there's no outcome evident—beware! Their true leadership identity lacks substance. They're fooling themselves.

Start Leading with Purpose Today

When your leadership identity has vitality, you can easily do the work of making your purpose clear wherever you are working. You can do this clearly stating the outcomes *you* expect at the start of things—and then making certain that those expectations are met or exceeded.

This applies to phone calls, meetings, teleconferences—in fact, to every leadership moment. Great leaders constantly ask themselves whether the outcomes they expect in those moments are those they want to be known for having achieved. It's applying The Rule. They first ask whether they meet the standards they hold for themselves. That's how they create the link between leading in any moment and achieving their true leadership identity.

You can start this immediately. Clarify your expectations at the start of every leadership moment, and ask yourself if they fit *your* standard—what *you* want to be known for as a leader. If your answer is: "Yes, but it's going to be a bit of a stretch," then you are probably in the right place. If your answer is: "Well no, not really," then you have to do something about it there and then. Otherwise you miss the opportunity to create the leadership identity you want and deserve.

So what can you do when the expected results are not up to snuff? There are a number of things you can do like deciding whether expecting more is possible and appropriate, asking people to raise their own expectations, or seeking out more competent or better-equipped people. You can even just say, "I am not satisfied that we're doing enough." There's always something more you can do.

CLEAR OUTCOMES

Leading My Self

Do I ensure that my expected outcomes are clear and consistent with my leadership identity?

Leading Others

Are we all clear on the outcomes expected of us and our personal accountability for delivering?

The job of achieving the great leadership performance you want and deserve is far more under *your* own management than you imagine. The key is to take the courageous step of engaging your true leadership identity in every moment.

Here's a quick quiz on the topic. Imagine you are preparing a presentation to be given to your organization. You sit down at your computer and start to prepare. Which is the most important question you should *first* ask?

(a) What do I want them to do as a consequence of hearing me speak?

(b) What knowledge do I want them to walk away with that they need?

(c) What do *I* want to walk away with that *I* did not have before the presentation?

They are all important, but which one should you ask first?

Here's a hint: Remember The Rule—first lead your self with excellence. The answer is (c): What you want to walk away with. It's also very often the most difficult to define.

Why this one first? Because it gives you a performance goal independent of your audience and puts you in the position of leading your self with excellence toward your leadership identity <u>before</u> you start to think about satisfying your audience. From that place you will craft a superb performance.

Constantly Reshaping Your Purpose

It takes hard leadership work to build a clear picture of intended outcomes that are aligned with your leadership identity. It's not a one-off or annual event. It's a constant process, usually conducted in the background, of clarifying your position and then seeking out and clarifying possibilities. The richer and stronger you make that image of the future, the more power and confidence you will have in each of your leadership moments as you put it into practice. Focusing on outcomes and thinking about their consequences is one of the best ways to make (and keep) that image strong.

Try the exercise that follows. It asks you to identify the outcomes you expect for your organization, for your team, for those who depend on your organization, and for yourself in three different categories— Now, If all goes well, and When you amaze yourself.

For maximum impact, repeat the exercise with members of your Board of Directors and with your team. It will strengthen your resolve. The important thing is to find the means of expressing your leadership identity through *results* rather than by *feelings*.

All these future outcomes you imagine are events in a life that *you* will be living. There is nothing limiting you but the choices you make in your leadership moments. You can choose to be satisfied with what you are achieving now, or you can choose to expect and do more. You can use your determination to push beyond outcomes that feel like a stretch. You *can* make that BIG difference.

Outcomes That Make a BIG Difference

Identify the outcomes you could achieve if you chose to make a BIG difference. Use your journal.

Outcomes For...	Now	If all goes well	Amaze yourself
Your Organization: *(Results like profits, sales, quality, output, production)*			
Your Team: *(Team member careers, health, compensation, relationships, safety)*			
Dependents: *(Like customers, suppliers, partners, consumers, community)*			
Your Self: *(Like career, family, wealth, recreation)*			

Complete this exercise by starting with the "Now" column and writing out two outcomes you are expecting under each heading. Then move to the next column, "If all goes well," and work down, and then to the third column. Remember that outcomes need to be tangible, measurable accomplishments.

CHAPTER EIGHT

Get Serious About Growing

W hat's been happening as you have looked through the lenses? If you have been looking at your situation truthfully, with that ready-to-transform-things state of mind, you probably will have picked up a number of basic insights into how your leader within is impacting your current situation. Other leaders have said things like:

> *Our goals have been shifting so much since we established them. How do I lift my people toward a shifting target?*

> *I struggle with other people's influence over me. How do I filter the messages down to the essential few?*

> *I feel like I'm constantly unable to play to my strengths. What do I need to do to stay on a firmer platform?*

> *Often, I can't find the determination to stay the course. Why does my drive sometimes disappear?*

> *On many occasions I'm stressed and far from clear about my purpose. How do I find clarity in those circumstances?*

Notice that these kinds of insights have a need attached to them in the form of a determined follow-up question.

Lenses aren't a one-shot deal. The more you use them to focus your leader within on a given situation, the more you distill insights down to specific items that need your focused attention.

Some insights you get are obvious and straightforward, like "That's going pretty well for me," or "I need to get those relationships sorted out," or "I need to get clear on the outcomes I'm expecting from my team." Others may be more of a positive or negative sensation like, "I'm pretty comfortable with my team's level of competence" or "It feels like my superiors don't support me enough." Perhaps your use of a lens awakens an old issue that's been lying unresolved for some time.

These are all examples of your leader within becoming alert to the need to change your situation for the better.

You should be prepared for periods of confusion and deeper questioning. Answers often emerge quietly and steadily rather than in a flash. Remember, there are no one-size-fits-all answers on the journey of growing to achieve your leadership identity.

Staying In Balance

Before you act upon insights, think back to that analogy I made earlier about physical training. Any coach or trainer will tell you that in order to see continued results you must also learn how to keep your exercise program in steady balance.

There are many aspects to physical balance: being sure to train every group of muscles proportionally (imagine someone with a weightlifter's torso and a runner's legs); keeping skeletal balance when lifting weights to avoid injury; and, perhaps most important, finding a balance between rest and exercise. Muscles actually grow not during use, but during rest. And marathon runners don't sprint; they find a pace that carries them though the race to the finish line.

The reason should be obvious. Growth cannot be rushed. Someone who exerts him- or herself constantly will eventually become exhausted, disillusioned, injured or, most likely, all three. By the same token, taking too much rest between exercise periods will negate any positive effects.

It's the same with your growth as a leader. Being serious about growing as a leader means you must learn to keep your development work in balance as your insights lead naturally to trying out new ways of operating. And as you practice, you will discover that a deeper sense of confidence grows, along with a certainty that your journey is the right one.

If time becomes urgent, and you push yourself and your team too hard, you can damage your strengths rather than develop them. By the same token, if you are too reflective, seeing time as unencumbered by milestones you must meet, you will never improve much of anything.

This sense of balance—you might also call it pacing—is essential to effective development.

Balance With Your Team

There's another aspect to balance as well: balance with your followers. Remember that *they* are the ones who will turn your new insights into improved results. It's easy to overload them with your latest and greatest ideas for improvement, but beware of instituting frenetic changes. Many leaders fail from the tremors produced by too many good intentions.

GROWING WORK

Leading My Self — Am I moderating my own development work and avoiding frenetic change?

Leading Others — Are my team members demonstrating that I have them growing at a pace that expands confidence and results?

What you give your team and what you receive in return needs to stay in harmony. This is more than just giving direction and getting results. It is giving the best of yourself and, in return, receiving the joy of knowing that your followers are growing along with you as they give the best of themselves.

Leaders who do not understand the pace of their own and their followers' development get out of balance with their team. Inevitably, they and their team grow increasingly alienated. Remember that image of my leader within, rushing me faster and faster, taking on way too much, barely communicating, and about to be fired.

Applying The Rule requires your leader within to do the work of staying in balance. The subject comes up often. For the moment, remember to stretch—but not to the point of losing your balance or that of your team. If stretching is a constant struggle, how will others react as they try to follow you?

From Insight to Actionable Work

So what do you do once your leader within gets an insight? How do you get your determination revved up, decide to do something, and find the right something to do?

There are many places to turn for an answer. The first place to start is always to tap your own resources. Here are just a few:

1. **Trust Your Inner Compass:** Trust your gut, or intuition, to point you to the best way to proceed and go with it.

2. **Find Best Practice:** Most likely you are not the first to have these insights, so find more knowledgeable others within and—if possible—outside your organization who can transfer the essence of their know-how to you.

3. **Ask Your Board of Directors:** They will not only help you craft the best way to proceed but also provide an effective feedback system to sustain you.

Of course, you're now left with perhaps an even tougher question: Of all the ideas for improvement before you, which is the best? To answer that one, it's worth knowing the simple test of leadership growth work.

The Test of Growth Work

Don't let your leader within become so inspired that you take on useless activities. I recommend that you test whether any activity you undertake to improve your situation and advance you toward your leadership identity meets *all four* of the following criteria:

1. **Have a Clear Purpose:** The task you engage in must have a clearly articulated purpose that leads to greater results for your organization, your team, and your self. It is not merely an exercise for its own sake.

2. **Be Clearly Accountable**: The activity must have a defined and measurable expected outcome for which you are clearly accountable.

3. **Play From Strength:** The activity must use and stretch your own core strengths. It should never depend on your weaknesses for success.

4. **Build the Identity <u>You</u> Want:** The activity must reflect the standards you have set in your heart and mind for the leader you honestly want to become. This is the principle reason most development work fails—The Rule again.

If the action you undertake doesn't satisfy all four criteria, beware! Stop and return to the lens and your leadership insights for more guidance. It's all four or nothing. It's amazing how many efforts fail because they don't meet the standards of this simple test.

(If you've recently completed a performance evaluation and it includes a personal leadership development plan, go back and apply the four criteria to it.)

Know the Context before Jumping In

Any activity that meets these four criteria is a valuable one. It might involve learning new skills or enjoying new roles and stretch assignments. Or perhaps you've already been asked to take on a more important position.

But never let your leader within rush, out of balance, headlong at a new role. Many leaders, for example, let their leader within become blinded by the temptation of an offer of greater rank and compensation. They end up in a serious downward spiral.

Keep these two nuggets in mind before you jump in:

1. *Your leadership strengths are not a predictor of success in a leadership role.*

Be sure to investigate the *context* in which you'll have to apply them. Knowing the specific leadership context will help you be honest with yourself about exactly which of your strengths you'll need. Will there be organizational support for strengths you lack? Will the strengths of those around you complement your own? Are you clear on the results you will be accountable for producing as well as their deadlines? Being unaware of this—or cavalier about it—is how the mighty fall.

2. *Evaluate your leadership strengths according to your own criteria and leadership identity.*

It may be flattering to be told how good you are at something, but if you know in your heart you're not, you will end up struggling with weaknesses instead of drawing from strengths. Don't imagine that hope and good intentions are ever sufficient strengths.

Does that mean you should turn down challenging opportunities? Absolutely not. Think in terms of *leadership roles* rather than positions, titles, or even responsibilities. A new position—for example, head of sales—can take the form of many different leadership roles, depending on the organizational context. The more senior you are, the more you have control over that context.

Here's the final nugget:

3. *Accept a new position (or responsibility or title) only if you know you can shape the organizational context to achieve a purpose that fits your strengths and brings your true leadership identity to life.*

Otherwise, think very hard before jumping in. I know firsthand that the big title and compensation package can be the gateway to the Valley of Despair.

Avoid ending up in a position that requires changing aspects of yourself you know can't be changed. Successful leaders do not waste time in situations that require focusing primarily on their weaknesses. Imagine how this would look to their followers.

One president I saw completed a 360° feedback that indicated a weakness in making "charismatic" stand-up presentations. After a few hours of training, he took every opportunity to get to his feet and act like a completely unauthentic idiot in front of his people. Yet he was an outstanding communicator in writing.

Remember: Play *from* your strengths. True to The Rule, playing from your strengths means looking inward and being certain of the strengths you have. It means applying them to new situations, which in turn grows your strengths even more. Playing from your strengths doesn't mean ignoring your weaknesses. It means deploying those strengths that have yielded tangible outcomes for you and your team in the past, and carefully stretching yourself (remember, balance!) with those strengths into new leadership roles.

So what kind of weaknesses do I want you to work on? Only the ones that are *challenges* for your great strengths. For example, if you're a great motivator of groups, push yourself to solve your perceived weakness using ever larger groups; if you're great at accounting for things, keep expanding the complexity of things for which you're accountable. That's what playing from your strengths should be like. Steady development from your strengths should be a permanent principle embedded in your leader within.

And what if you find that you can't play from your strengths to overcome weakness? Should you go on repeating the errors of the past and head for failure? No. Get someone else to do those things for you that has the strength. That's why you're the leader!

Being serious about your growth means keeping balanced and doing those few things that stretch your core strengths and have the greatest impact on performance. If you do too little, you may never feel you're growing, and if you take on too much, you may crash in a whirlwind of frenetic activity.

Get your leader within serious about growing, but also stay in balance.

Fast-Track Liz

Liz was a super high-flying senior vice president for a not-for-profit organization. She'd always pushed to be more productive, get more done, get promoted—and she had been really successful at it, too. She pushed her team to achieve more and more each day. For Liz, success only lasted a few minutes before she was on to raising the bar and solving the next problem.

She was always looking for ways to do things—lots more things—and do them better. She saw every insight into her leadership performance as a problem to be solved immediately. Liz's hunger to get to the next level was no secret. She had been on the fast track and wanted to continue making career leaps. As soon as she started one job, she began looking for (and talking about) the next—with her eye trained on the CEO position.

All of a sudden, though, the rapid promotions stopped. Liz's team, already resentful of her propensity to take all the credit for its success, grew less productive. Morale declined, and Liz grew increasingly cantankerous. She told those around her she was desperately unhappy with her team and the whole organization. She wanted to move to another company. There was, she felt, no time to lose.

What happened?

The problem, as you may already suspect, wasn't her team. Constantly looking toward the next opportunity, Liz couldn't see that development needs time. She didn't fully understand that her strengths needed to stretch as she grew in her position. She had reached the limits of her natural talents.

In fact, such a leveling is often a signal that it's time to reevaluate and create a new leadership identity (and probably a new Board of Directors in support of it) that isn't defined solely by meteoric growth.

FAST-TRACK LIZ

<u>Liz to Self</u>

I must have more.

I'm good enough, what's the next job?

Pushing is the only way to succeed.

<u>Liz to Others</u>

"You'll do far better if you..."

"How soon can I get promoted?"

"We have to raise the bar."

<u>Is this you?</u>

Give people time to reflect on what they've learned before thrusting them into the next job.

<u>Positive Strength</u>

Desire to excel.

Let's listen to Liz's leader within— that is, what she's saying to her self. "I'm running as fast as I can down a corridor, looking left and right for new doors to open. Whenever I see one, I'm drawn by the challenge it represents. My energy surges. I take a quick breath, open the door, and run down a new corridor until another doorway emerges. Where have all the doorways gone? I'm still running, but there's no more doorways! Help!"

The doorways Liz looked for were new jobs, new teams, new homes, and new friends. She had to see a doorway along her path once in a while to convince her that she had a real purpose. Her leadership identity was too much about the doorways and not enough about where each corridor was headed. No wonder she became frustrated when they stopped coming her way! The frustration led to a breakdown in trust between her and her team. She felt like a victim and wanted to get out.

When Liz told me this story, I suggested to her that there was a light cord dangling over her head while she was hurtling down the corridor so intently, expecting doorways to appear. Instead, I said, she could just reach up, pull the cord, and the light would come on. Then her leader within would see that the corridor was just a trick of the shadows. With the lights ablaze, she'd see construction material all around her—she just has to take some time to *build* a doorway wherever she liked, and go through it to where *she* wanted.

Liz realized she had been relying too much on other people to create her doorways—and, by extension, her growth to her leadership identity. When you imagine that time is running out, you become its victim. Time wasn't running out for Liz—just the opposite. She was running away from time. Actually, there was time to build her team, time to achieve a promotion, and time to build her career. Liz now makes her own doorways—all of which lead toward her true leadership identity. Her team develops along with her. Whenever she feels like a victim of time, she just reaches up and turns on the light.

This is The Rule in action: In your leadership moments today, stop for a second, pull the cord, and see how much great building material there is around you. Be grateful that it's there and it's yours.

PART THREE

Great Leadership Using The First Rule

All these ideas about The First Rule of Leadership mean nothing if you don't translate them to a greater performance in the complicated reality of your own leadership position. So for this book, I've picked— and tested with clients—five common situations where applying The Rule will give you immediate benefit.

They are leadership moments where you need to:

- *Deploy a balanced attitude.*

- *Create a great impact.*

- *Navigate the Valley of Despair.*

- *Let go of useless attachments.*

- *Energize a great team performance.*

I know these are just a few of the many situations where you will be challenged. No matter what the leadership situation, it all comes down to this: In each and every leadership moment, have The Rule firmly implanted in your mind, and make certain you are being the leader you want to be remembered for. Don't over-strategize situations. Lead your self with excellence and the greater outcomes you want and deserve will follow.

CHAPTER NINE

Deploy a Balanced Attitude

Some things knock me off my well-balanced leadership platform really fast. One of them is being asked a question loaded with sarcasm. It usually happens when I'm giving a talk about leadership and someone, usually at the end of the talk, asks something mocking like: "So what's the definition of a leader, anyway?" And then he launches into promoting his own self-serving views in front of his colleagues. My immediate reaction is to say something unprintable. I have to work to get myself composed and give a sensible answer that doesn't come from that bad-attitude place in me.

Can you relate to these kinds of things in yourself? Perhaps there are people or comments that trigger you to get irritated, angry, resentful or even just plain silent.

You know the reason that questioner triggers that response in me, don't you? It's got nothing to do with the question or the questioner. It's this: That bad attitude in me comes from the fact that I hate that part of me that enjoys doing the same thing at the end of other people's talks. And because I hate *myself* when I do it to others, I already know how to hate it when it's done to me. (Now that I've told you that, try expressing the things that get to you in the same way.)

Clearly it's important for me, when I'm leading a group like that, not to let that bad-attitude part come out and pollute the good things I'm trying to achieve. My leader within has to do the work of preventing me from tripping myself up. It's an example of what I mean when I say my leader within is working to keep me on my *well-balanced platform*.

By the way, my answer to the question "What's the definition of a leader, anyway?" is usually this:

> ***Leaders are those who can create a compelling picture of greater success for their organization and who also have the ability to lift the hearts, minds, and actions of people toward it.***

> ***But the fact is that when a leader can't manage her inner self in line with that picture, she undermines her credibility, destroys loyalty, and severely compromises performance.***

We see awful and extreme results of this on a grand scale in the public arena—priests defrocked, politicians impeached, and CEOs indicted. The Rule remains true no matter what the scale.

How You Think Impacts Your Team

Back to the important topic of keeping and—wherever you need to—deploying a balanced attitude.

When *you* are in the role of leader, everyone around you makes the decision, consciously or unconsciously, to follow or not follow you on your journey. Your performance is under their microscope. How you think about your job, how you behave, how you show what you feel, what you say, and what you stand for are all important to people in learning to understand and trust you. This applies even when they are at a distance, geographically, ideologically, or organizationally. You are far from being their sole source of information about their world, but what they hear, see, or feel about you and the way you lead your self will be key ingredients in their outlook. Do you think all the other people in my talk would ask their important questions if I transmitted my irritated response to that sarcastic questioner?

At the most basic level, being "watched" by others is very helpful for your leadership. If you are truthful, fair, and balanced with yourself, they know you will be the same with them, or at least they'll give you the benefit of the doubt. If you are confident in times of peril, they will be confident, too. When you judge them, they will try to understand how you judge yourself. When they sense the humor and compassion you have for yourself, they'll know that some will be available for them when they need it.

Again, this does not mean that you are the *exclusive* source of people's impression of their leader—how can that be for leaders of organizations with hundreds or thousands of people? But understand that your followers will *always* draw far more from your **core attitude**—how you feel in your innermost place about a topic—than from your words. They will talk about it in your absence, compare it with theirs, adopt it as their own, and, most important, seriously consider whether it helps or hinders them in achieving what they want.

So getting *your* core attitude in the right place can be critical to them achieving *their* results. It's The Rule again: *To get others adopting the attitude that produces the best outcome for them, first get your own attitude in the right place.*

In fact, the attitude you have as the leader can sometimes cascade through an organization faster than the speed of light. That's why you must try to stay balanced—unlike Carla.

Caring Carla

Before I got into leadership coaching, I always imagined that the worst kind of leadership attitude was exhibited by the macho Angry Bastard type of Rogue. I saw plenty of it in my early years in the organization that fired me. But that was before I met Caring Carla. In some ways she was just the opposite. She cared too much for everybody in her organization. And that produced a drop in performance as fast as any Angry Bastard's I've ever seen.

It was astonishing to see how quickly her core attitude propagated throughout her entire organization. True to The Rule, without balance, her team's attitude and performance started to take on her own. The team's purpose shifted from achieving hard business results to making sure that one another's cares were satisfied.

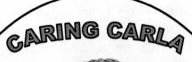

CARING CARLA

Carla to Self

I feel successful when
I please others.

How can I give more of
myself to them?

If I care enough, they
will like me and
follow.

Carla to Others

"I don't want to
add stress, but..."

"Can I do more to
help you?"

"Don't worry about
things, we'll get
there."

Is this you?

Success is not determined by your degree
of empathy but by results.

Positive Strength

Empathy for people.

When customers started to complain about late deliveries and quality, they were met with a barrage of nice intentions but no results. When some employees' benefits were paid late, they were simply asked not to worry. The owners eventually had to call a halt. She was loving their business to death.

Together with Angry Bastard, she became one of the founding members of the Gallery of Rogues. Don't be like her. When your team sees your core attitude, let them see someone who can balance caring with the need to deliver results.

Did you pick up on how Carla's over-caring attitude spread throughout the organization? There's the same cascade effect with the *right* attitude, too. Unfortunately it never flows as fast. And it needs constant repeated reinforcement.

There's another important message to mention briefly in association with this: You need to understand and defend yourself against those forces that could diminish your spirit. A negative spirit—perhaps brought on by your own stress or the skepticism of others—nourishes those who prefer not to see your (and often their own) true potential. Organizations are full of those who would prefer you to focus on criticizing people's failings rather than encouraging their success. I'll risk a bet that you already know a few of them. They're doom triggers. If you can, limit the extent to which they erode your core attitude. Your Board of Directors can really help when they do.

(The word "spirit" in this context needs clarification. Please don't think that this means religious. To a leadership coach, spiritual people are those who know how to connect to the highest inner power available to them as they go about their leadership work. This means accessing more of that part of you that identifies with the greatest good—the really positive aspects of your leadership identity. Your spirit is constantly shining out toward the people around you in very practical ways. It is your means of inspiring yourself and others to the greatest good. When you access that place, leading feels much easier—more like rolling downhill than battling to get to the top.)

Beware the Chitchat

Your spirit needs your attention in all your leadership moments. Imagine you're on your way to a meeting and someone corners you in the hallway to give you upsetting news. After you part, you find yourself carrying the resulting attitude with you, as though all the energy created by the interaction were still churning in your mind.

Or have you ever had someone constantly interrupt you when you're trying to get your point across? At the last interruption, your irritated response can't be suppressed any longer and you completely forget your point and start analyzing just why you let all that happen to you.

It's easy to let that private *chitchat* going on in your head get control of you. You know how it sounds—things like: "I should, I ought, I can't, I must," and "they should, they ought, they can't, they must," and so on. A lot of these thoughts are triggered from a pretty deep place, and they influence your attitude a great deal.

So if you bumped into someone else just after that hallway interaction, or if someone else was watching you get interrupted, he would see the result of all that chitchat going on in your mind. It would be in your expression, in your eyes and in your body language. Whatever your chitchat may be, another person would pick up on the resulting core attitude, and he would respond accordingly.

It's human nature to try to assess the attitudes of those we interact with. That's exactly what happens when you address an individual or a group. They're as interested in how you feel about what you are saying as they are in what you're saying. Like me and my response to that sarcastic question, showing the wrong emotion—whatever the chitchat it comes from—starts your listeners' chitchat going. It establishes the wrong communication pattern, sometimes without a single word being spoken.

Managing this transfer of attitudes is a crucial task for your leader within. Why?

> *As a leader, your core attitude at the beginning of all interactions is a big determinant of any outcome you get.*

And your core attitude in the middle and at the end of these interactions can seriously damage your ability to achieve your purpose if you don't manage it well.

Think about attitudes in your team while using this lens.

```
                  ATTITUDE  TRANSFER

        Leading My Self              Leading Others

        Am I deliberately and      Are attitudes within and
       consistently working to       around my team and me
        manifest the balanced          productive and
        attitude I expect of             respectful?
             others?
```

An investment in learning how to keep a balanced attitude when it's needed has a very high payoff in enabling a great performance from your team.

The View From the Balcony

Imagine you're watching the following cast of characters from a balcony seat in a theater:

A sales vice president of an engineering company is walking in the hallway. His boss has just beaten him up (figuratively) over some financial numbers. He goes directly from the conversation with his boss into a meeting with his team. He makes an angry, sarcastic comment about results, and one of his team members leaves the room in anger. The meeting comes to an abrupt halt.

What was the cause of the poor meeting? Was it (a) the fact that his boss spoke to him angrily, which then made him angry; or (b) his boss spoke to him and his own chitchat got (and kept) him miserably angry?

You're right: It was the chitchat.

Here's another example, with a few more ingredients. Keep your balcony view.

Ronnie, the CEO of an energy company and a highly intelligent person—a supercomputer mind—enters his monthly team meeting. Before everyone is seated at the table, he launches into a description of the state of the business and what needs to be done, detailing every element across all departments. He is a brilliant speaker with exceptional mastery of the details of his business. He talks nonstop as everyone else rushes to the table to take notes. And then he stands there, coffee mug in hand, and *keeps* talking. This supercomputer has to deliver all its data.

Occasionally, someone looks up from taking notes with an intellectually earnest expression. At other moments, colleagues raise eyebrows at one another across the table. (Chitchat: "Here he goes again!") He speaks nonstop for 20 minutes, delivering his detailed analysis of everyone's division along with his ideas and directives, before coming to an abrupt halt. Then everyone in the room is silent and left totally bewildered about what to do next. Most are still trying to digest the impact of the first few things he mentioned, and hoping the next bombardment of data will not be directed at them.

How did someone so smart get everyone confused so quickly?

From your view in the balcony, what would you say was his core attitude when he started, and what kind of chitchat was going on in his mind to create it? Would you predict his attitude of superiority at the beginning of a meeting would extend throughout the meeting? Since this is a true story, I can tell you that the meeting went downhill from there. His team members hardly contributed during the full day meeting, two of them nodded off, and there was no group decision-making or commitment. He didn't call a break for three hours, so you can probably picture the discussion in the rest rooms, too.

His core attitude at the beginning set him on the wrong course, and he ended up with the wrong outcome. There were signs everywhere of disrespect and mistrust for someone who, in reality, was extremely capable and talented. Ronnie's chitchat told him that he needed to be master of every detail and have every answer on every occasion in order to lead effectively. Was he out of balance? As a CEO, definitely.

From your position in the balcony, can you create the way you would have preferred Ronnie's meeting to start? You can rewrite the play this way: Start with the attitude and outcomes you want Ronnie to achieve with his team by the end of the cameo. Then picture Ronnie—still the same brilliant person—coming into the meeting with the attitude and approach that produces your envisioned outcome.

And while you're still watching from the balcony, picture the start of the last meeting you ran on your stage. Are there any effects stemming from *your* attitude? Would a rewrite be a good idea?

Now come down from the balcony.

There's some good advice for your leader within in that example:

> **Start with an outcome you want and determine the best core attitude you will need to achieve it.**

Why start leading badly and then have to waste energy correcting your course?

Keeping the Core Balanced

"Core" means something at the very heart, at the very center, but also something of substance: something that if it lay outside the body, you could practically touch. We're all different, so it follows that everyone's core contains a unique set of elements—emotions, habits, loves, prejudices, and needs—that exist in different combinations.

The leaders in those stories on the stage didn't make a conscious choice about desired outcomes at the beginning. Their core attitude was the result of habitual internal chitchat, and that led them the wrong way. They immediately fell off their balanced leadership platform. Worse than that, their leadership was driven by whatever chitchat happened to be going on at the moment. Without applying The Rule and governing their core attitude, they constantly gambled with their team's desire and ability to follow.

How do you get to the right attitude? And how can every one of your leadership moments have a good chance of working out the way you would like?

The answer is to try to tune in to your own core attitude and people's likely reactions *before you start things*. That gets your leader within onto a balanced, confident platform.

Then whenever your chitchat leads you to a place where you fall off your platform through anger, fear, arrogance, or intimidation, you know you are leading your self and your followers in the *wrong* direction, and you must stop and try to put yourself right. I dread to think of how many meetings I botched up as CEO by not applying this simple suggestion.

Another idea is to create your own ritual for getting centered. Some leaders try quick affirmations to get themselves there while others try to take a break and get some fresh air. Some choose to find a quiet place to pray or meditate.

One place I propose you go whenever you have the slightest doubt—before, during, or after a leadership moment—is back to the balcony in your mind's theater. But this time, look down on *yourself* on the stage. I call it doing mental **balcony work.** Picture the situation you are in, or are about to engage in, on a stage in a theater, then apply The Rule by first asking: How is this event helping us achieve our purpose (outcomes) and the ultimate leadership identity I want to create?

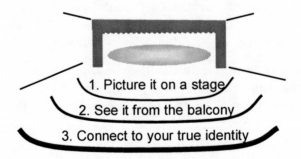

From this vantage point, you can see your own core attitude and the reaction of your followers. Let your intuition guide you from there.

But if ever you are in doubt, simply stop and apply our definition of your leadership purpose: It's about outcomes, not feelings. In any leadership moment, if it feels like your attitude has you losing your way, get clear on what has to be delivered. Unbalanced attitudes come back into balance when you focus on results. (Try this one out.)

The Attitude That Pays

What do you imagine would be the answer if you asked all your followers—past, present, and future—this question: If they could pick just one core attitude for you to show, one they would like you to demonstrate on all occasions no matter what the circumstances, what would it be?

You might imagine they would say something like: "Ease up on us." In truth, most people never want that attitude in their leaders. They *want* to be challenged. What they do say when asked are things like: "Willingness to help us on our journey," "Making things clear so we can succeed," "Involving us so we understand," "Listening to our opinions," and "Helping us grow." In short, they want your core attitude to be *compassion* toward them. When you come from a place of compassion toward the world, including those you lead, and you keep your eye on results, things seem to flow in the right direction. Don't confuse this with being a Caring Carla—this is compassion with an eye on results not feelings.

Take a moment now to climb back up to the balcony and see yourself exhibiting compassion for people in your team and your organization. Can you see that things will play out differently with this more compassionate approach?

Two Steps to Finding Compassion

As someone who has struggled to master how to respond to the sarcastic question, I can tell you that it takes discipline to create a momentary space within yourself when you know your core attitude is out off kilter. In that moment of deciding to put my chitchat aside, I try to detach and look down from above (yes, from the balcony) on the situation I'm in and *choose* how my leader within will govern it.

Working with many leaders I've discovered that it helps to see this as a two-step process. The first step is to give up, or ***surrender***, your old chitchat-produced core attitude completely. Sometimes I say something simple under my breath like, "I give up my need to shove that question back down his throat" and I keep saying it to myself until the feeling passes.

The second step is to then ***replace*** it. I try to think about my Fish—becoming a great coach—and that gives me the attitude I need. Replacing with compassion is best, but I can't always find it in my mind. Compassion toward others, of course, comes from finding *compassion toward your self* in that moment of detachment, from that seat in the balcony, just after that moment of surrender. Finding a little kindly sympathy for my leader within and letting it flow out to those around me is hard leadership work.

When you study great leaders, you see they've learned the right way to govern their attitude in every moment—often with the simplest conscious thought. It seems like there's always a position that they come to that foretells a great outcome.

This is definitely something to be learned and perfected along your leadership journey. This choosing to surrender your wrong core attitude in favor of a better one is how you put The Rule into action. Each time you try to do it, you are leading your self well, no matter how hard it is to move something into its place.

Are you comfortable committing yourself to using the "balcony," "compassion" and "surrender and replace" concepts to manage your core attitude? If not, explore why for a moment. Are those reasons valid? Remember our definition of leadership purpose: It is results, not feelings. If feelings like fear (of abandoning a comfortable attitude) or insecurity (in displaying compassion) are holding you back from producing results, you should think again.

Manage Your Attitude

Leading the Self Well

1. Think of leaders who clearly <u>don't</u> lead themselves well. Ask yourself if you would be willing to follow them. Is there a correlation between their attitude and how much you trust them? Between their attitude and your willingness to follow?

2. What about members of your Board of Directors? How well do (or did) they lead themselves? How did they, and you, cope with occasions when their attitude was far from helpful?

Chitchat

1. Relax for a moment and let your mind focus, one by one, on members of a team in which you're a member, not a leader. As you examine each individual, notice the chitchat that surfaces.

2. Repeat the exercise, and think about people on a team you lead. Try suppressing strong negative chitchat about people's performance or attitude toward you. How easy is it for you to put the chitchat on hold and create a clean slate?

3. Recall a leadership moment where your negative chitchat caused you to begin with an unproductive core attitude. How would you replay that moment now?

Take a look at those people in your organization who never seem to govern themselves well, who take great pride in believing that their core attitude never needs to be balanced or well managed. Or who simply lack the consciousness to manage themselves in the moment. We see them everywhere—those who take a two-dimensional view of the world, never trying to adapt themselves to achieve the greatest outcomes. They never realize how much more they can achieve. They make the same mistakes repeatedly on their journey.

Unlike you, none of them ever consider how much they can improve their chances of success by deploying their attitude using The Rule.

CHAPTER TEN

Create a Great Impact

Soon after I lost my job and was passing through the Valley of Despair, I was very fortunate to get my first CEO coaching client. I found him to be friendly, ambitious and eloquent, and very intent on creating a big difference with his executive team. As we explored the ideas behind The Rule and Total Leadership, he suggested that I meet with his team and get a broader perspective so he could improve their team meetings.

The executive team members shocked me. It was a complete hodgepodge. The leader they described was entirely different from the one I had met. One said he was an inspiration while another found him to be a tyrant and overcontrolling. Another said he lacked knowledge and was incapable of making good decisions, while another said he was the best problem-solver she had ever met. I started wondering which version of him I would bump into next.

Of course I figured out quickly that none of the versions of him, including my own, was the truth. And although he described his style as one thing, he was actually being experienced as someone, or rather a hodgepodge of someones, quite different.

Simply put, he had no sense of the picture of himself that he was creating in the minds of people. They were all responding to a different person. No wonder his team meetings were unproductive.

Your leadership style can inhibit rather than accelerate performance you get from your team. Shouldn't you, therefore, care how your team experiences you?

Style vs. Impact

Think about the impression—or better, the natural *impact*—you make on people as you lead. Be clear on this: Impact is not a synonym for style. It's the *result* of your style as expressed in the attitude, thinking, and actions of your followers. It is the version of you that others are reacting to as you are leading.

Let's look at it the other way around. Imagine you are working alone in your office, and your boss is on the other side of a glass-paneled door. You begin to hear his muffled voice, and turn to look through the glass. What you see is the person pictured here—your boss—coming toward you. What might you expect from the encounter? Would your chitchat tell you he'll be pleasant and well mannered? Quiet or loud? In a hurry or relaxed? Interested in you or himself?

Before he speaks, you might expect that he's angry about something—or at you. So by the time the door flies open and he comes in, you would have your usual here's-the-angry-boss response at the ready.

(Yes, it's the founder of the Gallery of Rogues—Angry Bastard.)

This person doesn't feel he's acting angrily. In fact he believes his style is forthright, passionate, and direct. You experience his impact as anger, and your defense to anger comes into play. The meeting begins with miscommunication, and any chance of achieving the best result is lost. It usually rolls downhill from there.

Your Leadership Impact

Back to you and your impact. You know yourself from the inside out. Others know you from the outside *in*. You may imagine that you are naturally a motivator and inspirer of your followers, but they may well experience you as the opposite.

ANGRY BASTARD

AB to Self

I'm so passionate
and direct.

Am I the only one
determined?

Why can't they just
<u>do</u> it?

AB to Others

"What the hell is
going on?"

"I want a lot more
action out of you!"

"You lack urgency.
Get going!"

Is this you?

Your anger floods situations. Practice
detachment or let steam off elsewhere.

Positive Strength

Drive and energy.

Think about the collision course that Angry Bastard is on.

Collision Course

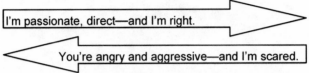

I'm passionate, direct—and I'm right.

You're angry and aggressive—and I'm scared.

It comes down to this: Do you want to create an impact where your followers are inspired to deliver fantastic results? If you do, then you can't simply leave your impact to chance. You have to apply The Rule to get your impact working for you rather than against you in shaping achievement.

Leadership Impact

The leader your followers respond to. The effect you have on their actions, thinking, and spirit.

Picture your leadership impact working this way in any leadership moment: What you're thinking—including all the chitchat—filters through your personality and habits, and reveals itself as action. Your followers see that leadership action—the expressions on your face, your spirit, your body language, what you say—and interpret its meaning based on *their* understanding of you. Then they react to you based on *that* interpretation. If they react to you in a way that enables and motivates them to improve outcomes, then you have achieved your purpose. If they act in some other way, despite your intentions, your impact has led them in an unintended direction, away from your leadership purpose.

Reminder: The Rogues in this book are all examples of leaders whose admirable core attitudes and strengths motivate people in the wrong direction by creating the wrong leadership impact. Again, the Rogues are all gender neutral.

You've probably already realized that you have the potential to appear like an Angry Bastard or any other of the Rogues you've met. I'll even go so far as to guarantee that when you're under *stress*, one or more of them come into play. At the very least, you should uncover and master any such impact defects that you create (or have already created) that can undermine your ability to enable a great performance in your team.

Leadership Models

Some organizations try to support their leaders by defining explicit "leadership models" to help executives understand the behaviors that generate the right kind of impact. These can be extremely valuable in translating important leadership values into actions. But as with all such tools, it's important to recognize that in real life, there is no such thing as a model leader. Perhaps you've been told that you have a style that emanates from a particular personality type. You may have learned that there are certain postures or speaking techniques that can improve your style.

Use these tools. They are good at creating insights into your impact, but only if you're sure they'll help you to achieve your purpose (outcomes) *today* with your team. Don't use them for their own sake. Always take your new understanding for a test drive in a leadership moment, and then feel free to "adopt, adapt, or abandon."

One important caution: These models compare you to a composite of other people's talents. This tempts you to devalue your own strengths. If you project that core attitude to your followers, imagine what they would do. The Rule suggests that they will devalue their own strengths—and eventually devalue you as a leader. Compare—yes; devalue your own strength—never. I've seen too many leaders stunted because not achieving the defined "ideal" undermined their self-confidence.

Getting Feedback on Your Impact

People say that there are two major problems with feedback. One is giving it and the other is getting it. In fact, feedback is a gift when it's done right. It's essential to your leadership journey because it brings you the power of an outside perspective.

It's difficult to be able to gauge your own impact across the entire range of personalities on your team. You can recognize extreme responses, but understanding and acknowledging the full extent of your impact is best done through a feedback system that gives you information you can trust.

There are many valuable systems available to collect and analyze information from people. And with a repeat of that caution about comparing your self to "model" leaders, I would suggest three important conditions for any feedback system you employ.

1. **Context:** The information should be given to you in a shared and balanced context of trying to achieve your purpose—improved results—by someone you trust and to whom you feel accountable.

2. **Description:** It must express your impact in terms of expanding or limiting the achievement of improved results by your followers. It should not express hearsay, feelings, or casual observations.

3. **Follow-through:** It should focus you on the specific context in which you lead so that you can immediately make *small* adjustments in your leadership behavior to see improved outcomes.

If you can't satisfy these conditions, beware of the feedback system! You will do much better if you take a few private moments with colleagues or followers and simply ask these questions:

What are the things I do that help you make a big difference?

What are the things I do that get in your way?

Try asking these First Rule questions today. You'll see how they build your confidence and accelerate getting the important things accomplished.

Adapt Your Impact to Get Results

You may think that discovering and managing your impact may sound unnecessary—even downright deceptive—if you believe that your "true" personality must shine through in every situation. But leading your self with excellence means that many times you have to sacrifice *your* needs in favor of *theirs.* Your followers need to see their way to achieving great results for themselves. So don't let your "true" personality (which may, in fact, be no more than a familiar, habitual mode of behavior) interfere with the process of genuinely inspiring people, helping them stay aligned with your goals, and performing well on their own journeys.

Does that really make you disingenuous? Consider this example: A client of mine was baffled that his team seemed downright hostile to him. Strange, he thought, because he considered himself admirably forthright: someone who expressed his true feelings all the time, without holding back. On one occasion, he told his gathered team members that he didn't like some of their spouses. On another, he told his customers that he had been in a physical fight with his sister. Though these things were true, it should come as no surprise that revealing them damaged his leadership impact. His team didn't need to know the truth for their own sake; they needed him to help them realize their own leadership purpose. His customers didn't need to know his private affairs, they needed him to provide a great product and service. What's worse, he delivered the "truth" with a total lack of dignity. You can predict the outcome.

You have to engage your leader within to help you understand your impact and adapt your style to fit the circumstance. This does not mean letting go of your deeply held beliefs. Nor does it mean hiding important things from people. It is no great sacrifice to lead your self prudently so that those around you are free to pursue their purpose unencumbered. If your style causes your followers to fall out of balance, nobody wins.

Keeping the Impact Antenna Tuned In

Like most people, your followers can tolerate a broad range of managerial styles and still deliver good results. After all, you are not perfect, and every leader is entitled to make a mistake now and again. But that luxury doesn't extend to *repeating* the same mistakes over and over. Continuously projecting a style that impacts negatively on others will inevitably damage the image they have of you, until their performance is undermined no matter what the situation.

This perceived negativity impacts your performance like barnacles on a ship—they thrive in difficult circumstances, they slow you down and take you off course, and you have to divert to be rid of them.

The only answer is to keep your ***antenna*** tuned in so that you make the needed adaptation.

For example, think about how you would respond to the force of an Angry Bastard leader. Responding by adopting an angry core attitude, although tempting, only adds fuel to the fire. Hiding or ignoring achieves nothing. Instead, you must help him get his feedback antenna working again.

How do you that? You can try demonstrating through your actions how he should listen to you. You can redirect the conversation away from action and toward the principles and purpose behind what is to be achieved. Try asking, "What's our real purpose here?" rather than "What are you forcing me to do?" Try establishing new principles for your working relationship. Never ignore the situation— it will then just reoccur. Always try to get his antenna raised and tuned in.

And what does the Angry Bastard in you—or any other out-of-balance Rogue you resonate with—do if you're leaving a negative impact? After all, if your antenna is damaged then only a weak feedback signal can get through.

Apply The Rule and start leading your self. You can simply halt and wait. Doing nothing is highly underrated as a technique for pressing the ***adjust button***. Remember balcony work, compassion, surrender, and replace in the last chapter? You can also let those in front of you know that you feel you may be coming on too strong with what you are saying. You can ask for their help, too.

When your impact antenna is up, it's a lot like musicians working an audience. Great musicians give, and their audiences give back. Both rely upon an agreement between leader and follower. This agreement—consent given by applause or a nod of the head, a look on the face—is a sign that the purposeful flow of information between the leader to the follower can continue in the best way.

Acknowledge Where Your Impact Is Wrong

It's helpful to realize the difference between the *initial* and *developed* impact that people have toward you. Your *initial impact* is caused by the immediate, prewired responses of people when they first meet you or if they are meeting you again after a long period of time. You probably know about this from interviewing job candidates.

Your *developed impact* is the wiring that *you* create in people's minds. It is the image of your leadership that exists in their minds after multiple exposures to you. With repeated exposure to you and your leadership situation, your followers build their own comfortable picture of what they can expect from you—barnacles and all.

Consider the quietly spoken new president of one company. He quickly developed a weak impact among an aggressive and boisterous team. By his third leadership team meeting, he was running a circus. People were not fully listening and were interrupting him and diverting decision-making. He decided to use a trick he had seen as a schoolboy. At the start of his fourth meeting, he withdrew a large pocket watch and stared at it quietly for a moment. There was silence. He stared at the watch as the silence extended from seconds to minutes. After two minutes of silence he turned his gaze toward his team and at the top of his voice shouted "Sex!" Then he paused and said quietly, "Will you listen to me on *that* subject?"

The nervous laughter gave way to a much deeper realization. He was pressing the adjust button on his developed impact. At all future meetings he kept the watch on or near the table and he only had to look like he was reaching for it for the room to become silent and attentive. No more barnacles were going to stick to that ship. (Try it if your team stops listening to you.)

Reacting to Leaders' Impact

Create a list of four or five of the members of your Board of Directors (those that are not historical figures).

1. Think back to the first time you met each one of them. What was their initial impact upon you? What previous experiences got you hard-wired to respond to them that way? Were they in or out of balance?

2. Now think of their developed impact — the way you respond now. How different is the impact they have on you now from the impact they had initially? If different, what caused the change?

Close this exercise by picturing two leaders you took an instant dislike to. Recall the traits in them you despise. What was hard-wired in you to reject them so quickly?

Micromanager Mary

You may have met Micromanager Mary. She is a Rogue whose initial impact is extremely productive, yet her developed impact can be a disaster.

She is always very interested in making sure you're doing your job in *precisely* the right way. And that way, of course, is *her* way. That can be very useful when you're new to her team. You feel the satisfaction of getting through the initial learning period at top speed.

But it masks her true identity. As a follower, what you think, feel, or believe is of no concern to Mary. She *must* have things—including all the detail she loves to understand—done the "right" way. She's usually very smart; after all, she has to be able to do everyone else's job so well!

For her part, she believes that her knowledge of how to do things right is essential. Therefore she must tell her followers exactly how to do things in order to be successful.

But her impact antenna is badly damaged. It fails to pick up the signal that followers also need to learn for themselves, grow from their own strengths, and achieve leadership identities of their own.

She's not interested in finding a balance in her impact so that team members feel they are growing from their strength. Her way is the only path between A and B. That's why she complains so hard that there's nobody on her team that can be her successor. Are you a Micromanager Mary?

Just look at the collision course that Mary is on.

Collision Course

I know the best way—so do it my way!

You're cramping my style—and I don't like it.

Picture her message being transmitted time and time again. Is it any wonder that every Micromanager Mary complains about insufficient respect from her team and the loss of good people? She works extremely hard to build those responses into people.

MICROMANAGER MARY

Mary to Self

I have to get it
perfectly right.

I'm the only one that
knows how to do
things here.

Only idiots don't see
my way is best.

Mary to Others

"I'm unhappy: You're
not doing this right."

"Let's look at the
details of how it gets
done."

"You'll find my way _is_
better."

Is this you?

Give people a chance to find _their_ way
to perform and then praise them.

Positive Strength

Attention to
process/details.

Let the Lens Be Your Antenna

If you're coming across as an Angry Bastard or a Micromanager Mary (or any other Rogue) and you want to change your impact, you have to start by accepting responsibility—perhaps for the first time in your life—for the role you play in the way people respond to you. You have to trust that your leader within can manage you to make a far better impact and develop relationships that inspire excellence.

You're not working in an environment in which you'll be appreciated under any circumstances. You need to manage your impact with people who are initially total strangers and who must decide, in a competitive world, whether or not to like you, to work with you, to accept your ideas, and to pursue your leadership identity with you. They often have little investment in you. It's up to you to show, in every leadership moment, that their faith in you is well founded. To some extent, you have to start afresh each time you meet. And unlike many personal situations, this environment requires that your impact be positive and respectful *all* the time.

Picture your own leadership performance and examine it through the impact lens. Remember to start with the question on the left.

```
                          IMPACT

        Leading My Self              Leading Others

     Am I doing all I can to     Is my team demonstrating
       keep my impact both          that my impact is
      inspiring and well           helping them achieve
            balanced?                   their goals?
```

Think hard about any insights that come up. Do you need to straighten out your confusion between style and impact?

Pressing the "Adjust" Button on Your Impact

In addition to getting feedback from your team, here are a few things you can do to purposefully manage your leadership impact in every leadership moment.

1. **Start with Your Spirit in the Right Place.** Get your self into the state of mind where you connect, and stay connected, to the greatest good, the really positive things that you and your team are trying to achieve.

2. **Know Your Purpose:** Be clear at the start of every occasion as to what outcomes you are trying to achieve, and how they relate to your team's purpose. When purpose is fully acknowledged, your impact always starts in a positive place.

3. **Practice Balcony Work:** Learn to see yourself and your impact from that higher altitude and make real-time adjustments in each leadership moment.

4. **Look Through the Leadership Lens:** Take the lens to your leadership moments and periodically pause and put it into action. Use it repetitively and let the insights keep emerging.

Imagine the adjustment to your impact if, at your next meeting, you didn't dive into the agenda but instead you started the meeting by taking five minutes for yourself to establish the impact *you* want. Perhaps in these five minutes you talk about the results of your organization, and remind everyone about the great value you are all trying to bring stakeholders, and then you honestly and positively describe some specific people's contributions. You'll be saying things such as: "I really like what Agnes is doing in Finance to speed up the weekly sales reporting," or "A new customer called me to say how pleased she is with Frank."

Would the positive news of your impact leak out of the meeting to people not in attendance? How about the effect on those you mentioned and praised that were not even there? After your five minutes is up, would the business part of the meeting start with people adopting the tone you want? (The best way to find out is to try it. Take that five minutes and see your impact start to change.)

Take Responsibility

So whose problem is it when your followers don't understand, don't listen, or go in the wrong direction? From coaching hundreds of leaders and their teams to success I have learned this about leadership impact:

> *The distortion between the leadership you want and the results you get is more your problem than theirs.*

Too many leaders complain about their team and say they don't "get it." Then they use the same excuse to dodge accepting their teams' feedback.

Managing your leadership impact is not as simple as exchanging one "style" for another. It requires focused work by your leader within to learn the sensitivity of managing your impact on others so that *they* are able to discover the greater performance that lies within them.

You can be sure of one thing: When you avoid applying The Rule and leave your leadership impact to serendipity, your team's performance will surely suffer. Occasionally, you'll be lucky. But if you don't engage your leader within to lead your self, you risk being dismissed as an archetypal out-of-balance leader who is ineffective, at best.

Take charge of your leadership impact now.

CHAPTER ELEVEN

Navigate the Valley of Despair

There's nothing like a sudden change to get your leader within agitated. You can move from normality to craziness overnight. The following questions will give you some perspective. Answer each one on a scale from "That never happens in my organization" all the way to "Yes, that's us to a tee!"

Has your organization experienced a huge disruption recently?

Is your organization undergoing a hiring freeze or major downsizing?

Is it tough for you or your colleagues to get motivated each day and sustain momentum? Are you and others feeling just plain miserable on many days?

Are conversations with colleagues far more about the politics of surviving than the future success of the organization?

Do you and your colleagues sacrifice a lot of personal time to work harder—yet fail to make headway?

Are people quitting even though, from your viewpoint, things have started to turn around?

If you answered, "That never happens in my organization" to *all* the questions, then skip this chapter: You're in heaven. Otherwise, get a handle on what craziness means by listening in on this informative (and true) conversation as Paul, a leader at a bank, speaks to a small audience about the terrible events of September 11, 2001. Paul is a senior leader whose offices were very close to the World Trade Center.

Paul's Story

"You all know what took place on 9/11. On our side of the building, we heard the first explosion but couldn't see it. We then heard the second explosion, and things went very quiet. My wife called me from her office on the other side of the Hudson; she could see everything from across the river. She screamed at me to get out. I opened the emergency fire exit for the second time in my life. (The first time was nine years before. Our previous office was high up in the tower that was bombed.) I opened up the door, and we all ran down 22 flights of stairs and into the street. It was only then that I could see what had happened. The 103rd floor—my former office—was hit.

"My knees just buckled and I sank down and started crying. Someone next to me out on the street started to cry, too. I was dazed and confused. Just after that, I told myself that I needed a plan of action. A plan came to mind—get home, see my wife, have dinner, and be grateful for being alive. That's what I decided to do. What followed was a 10-hour journey, some of it in a police car, to get home to my wife.

"Our business was devastated when the building it was in collapsed at the end of that day. Things were completely crazy. How could we continue our work? Our backup computer systems at another site were far from perfect. We began seriously doubting our ability to lead the business. Our self-confidence had collapsed, too.

"Although we were down, people wanted to try getting on with something good—anything to stop the constant worrying. The act of creating something snowballed. People came together using the telephone and the Internet to create new ways to keep our business running. We just focused ourselves, one day at a time, on moving forward.

"This ended up being the best way to deal with all the grief and anger that emerged over the coming weeks. It still comes up periodically, even though we have settled into our new offices.

"There was another feeling, too, the feeling of, "Why me? What did I do wrong? Could I have avoided it? Why did it all happen to me?" We talked about this a great deal, but it seemed to get us nowhere. I finally concluded that it rains on us all at some time, and you just have to deal with it and move on to the next place without needing to understand all the causes.

"The other thing I got out of this was how important it is to remember what you've already achieved on your journey. In adversity, when things are going crazy, it's very easy to forget all the good stuff that you managed to create, particularly with your team. You're not devoid of ability, even though you end up questioning it seriously. When we focused on our strengths, it made us all realize that we <u>can</u> use them in order to get through."

The Valley of Despair

You've heard some of my story of being fired. Do you have a similar one? One in which your leadership identity suddenly felt like it was lost? Anybody who's been downsized, reorganized, or just plain "improved" experiences these feelings to a greater or lesser extent. These are moments when your confidence and commitment to your leadership identity are severely tested.

The dramatic moments described in Paul's story show the stages that the leader within passes through when a major change knocks us off course and into craziness:

1. Initial shock as events hit, when, metaphorically, our knees buckle and we become disoriented.

2. A sinking feeling as sadness comes upon us and we realize that our world has changed permanently. The leadership purpose we were pursuing is falling in tatters as we seek to know more, often fearing the worst.

3. Uncertainty about what to do. Just wanting to get through each moment by finding productive activities and moving in a positive direction.

4. Questioning events, sometimes even blaming ourselves for being involved—why they happened to us, and how we might have done things differently to avoid the pain.

5. Finally, rediscovering our core strengths and drawing upon them to create a different identity—a new Fish—that draws us to a new, hopefully better, destination.

This is what it's like to pass through the Valley of Despair. Such life-changing external events happen to every leader occasionally, to most people many times, and to some leaders constantly. You should expect them. It's what you do as you pass through the valley that counts. Look at the following examples:

Two Trips Through the Valley

Chris

Chris was the general manager of an electronics business. He was listening to a local radio station on the way to his office one Monday morning when he heard that his company had been purchased over the weekend. When he arrived at work, a representative of the new owner intercepted him and told him he was no longer needed. The person calmly explained Chris's severance package and wished him well.

Half an hour after losing his job, the severance was not the issue. Chris's feelings were. He was entering the Valley of Despair. His leadership journey felt like it had suddenly petered out, and he imagined his career might be over. "All the years of service, the tough leadership decisions, the worrying about the business and the people," Chris lamented, "just to end up like this." And then, "Where did I go wrong?"

Yet three months later he was enjoying his new job as CEO of a non-profit company. What happened?

Sally

Sally, a senior manager in a large R&D organization, learned late one Friday morning that her department would be merged with another one and to expect major layoffs. Her immediate concern was for her family. As the primary breadwinner, she wanted to know just where she stood. At the company meeting that afternoon, she took the bold step of asking for more information. She was told that there would be further announcements over the coming weeks but, as yet, no details had been decided.

What followed for Sally was a tortuous period of corporate indecision in which her future was in constant flux. The great work she had done in building her team started to unravel under the strain of an extremely fuzzy future. "Why can't they listen to us down here?" she would say, "We're the ones that have to get the product developed that's needed to boost sales. Yet we're the ones being downsized. They're nuts!" She and her team were constantly having their hopes built up and then let down. It was a roller-coaster journey through the valley.

Two months later, she was head of her department. What happened?

A Closer Look

To begin answering what happened to Chris and Sally, consider this: Why are we discussing a "valley" and not just a plain old descent into despair?

Recognize that when these dislocating events occur during your leadership journey, your leader within feels an immediate loss of control of your leadership identity. It feels like your future is shot.

In fact that's not true. You're beginning a period of change toward a new place where the identity you can create is not yet clear. Although you may not be able to see the next point on your leadership journey, there is something you can do immediately.

> *You can decide, no matter where you have been, that the next part of your journey will be even better.*

That is, your leader within can choose to let these events move you onward and upward rather than backward and downward. That makes the period of despair actually a time of discarding outmoded aspects of your self so that you emerge from the valley with a leadership identity readjusted to reflect new circumstances.

You Will Lead Through Many Valleys!

Change is the true test of your leadership. You can expect a great deal of it on your journey. Whether it arrives by exceptional circumstance or whether you create it deliberately to improve your organization's performance, change generates strong forces within you and your organization. And you must learn to master both, starting, as The Rule says, with you.

The length and depth of the valley you pass through depends on how you manage your self through these times.

I know from hard experience that the following is simple to say, yet so difficult to do. When events occur beyond your control, you can choose to approach it as passing through a valley to higher ground or you can imagine that you're edging toward a slippery, perpetual downward slope. Without doubt, this choice is the work of your leader within.

If you come to expect that your journey will have its ups and downs, you can respect and appreciate the valleys for the opportunities they offer. However, if your leader within is not taking that more detached view then your journey can be a painful roller-coaster experience.

Just remember that ups are often preceded by downs. Expect them, and learn to anticipate them.

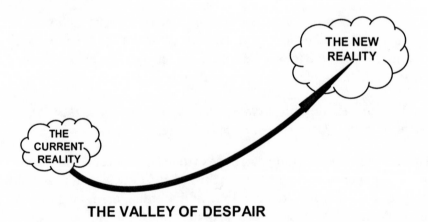

THE VALLEY OF DESPAIR

Passing through these times of change is inevitable. Not letting your leader within submit to the transitory feelings is what differentiates great leaders from mediocre ones. Remember former mayor Rudolph Giuliani on 9/11? You, too, are going to face many shocks (though hopefully not of that magnitude) on your leadership journey. Remaining determined to do whatever it takes to make a better future for you and your followers—despite how it feels—is the key.

Your Valleys of Despair

Look back over your life. What difficult events or circumstances caused you to pass through the Valley of Despair?

1. *Recall the different stages of one particular valley:*
   - *initial shock*
   - *period of sinking and self-doubt*
   - *desire to get through each moment*
   - *angry/blaming questioning*
   - *rediscovering core strengths*

2. *Have the valleys become any shorter or shallower as you have become older?*

3. *Can you recall any times when you consciously chose to see a valley as leading you ultimately somewhere better?*

4. *What relationships, places, opportunities, or actions helped you on the journey through your valleys?*

Finish by looking ahead three years. Based on the last three years, how many times can you expect to pass through the valley in this time period?

Your Change Capacity

The strength and resolve to lead your self and your organization to a better place in tough times is the power behind your capacity to deal with change. I'm talking about a core attitude that comes from within once the shock of change passes through you. It emerges at the point when you roll up your sleeves and say to yourself: "Okay, this stuff has happened to me, so what's next? What should I do right now for the good of myself and my team?" It's an inner spiritual call to action in the right direction, which counterbalances the fear, anger, and self-doubt you may still be feeling.

Have you ever experienced a leadership moment when things are changing and your resolve is called into action? You may have been singing in the chorus of complainers when suddenly a voice within said, "Why don't I try getting myself going in a better direction?" Or you may have been wallowing in pain and sadness, and something or someone you turn to triggers more determined thoughts like Paul's after 9/11. Your *change capacity* reveals itself to those around you by what you choose to do in that moment and thereafter.

When your change capacity is high, you come across as flexible and able to take the lead in changing situations. When it's low, you may find yourself described as "inflexible," "unfocused," "overreacting," and even "determined not to change." Either way it is a trait for you to understand, discuss with your Board of Directors, and develop.

Your change capacity develops steadily as you continue on your leadership journey. You may not notice this development, since it takes place inward. We all start with a capacity to handle change that we developed in our early years. But with each new experience we conquer, we learn how to manage our own psyche through major changes. Simply put, your change capacity develops by learning to deal with life's unplanned events. You can't learn this in a classroom. Neither should you expect to manage things perfectly on all occasions.

Maintaining the perspective of a journey is crucial. There are many events in life that are major, personal, and unexpected. They hit like the proverbial ton of bricks. It's simply unreasonable to expect such events to leave you unscathed. On the other extreme are the minor disruptions and imperfections experienced every day: people being delayed, computers not working, and cars breaking down. If you let these things hit you hard—into the valley—then you're in for a rough trip indeed.

Sure Will, Boss!

Remember that the valley occurs when your leadership identity—that vital mental and emotional picture of your future impact—undergoes a major loss. If you are to rebuild your leadership identity, it takes a little time to mourn the old you and create the new. This is a vulnerable time so it's easy to be susceptible to all sorts of people.

One person to avoid is Sure Will. You may think he's your savior, the best person on your team, but he can be lethal. He doesn't even flinch when faced with major obstacles. When there's a problem, he comes forward rolling up his sleeves when all other team members are struggling to find traction. He wants to get on and do work, any work, regardless of the outcomes. He can seem like an oasis in a desert of gloom.

But watch out! Sure Will doesn't experience any real loss because he's got nothing real to lose. He has no leadership identity and lacks any real purpose. He is not able to focus on results because he's blinded by his need to oblige. He'll take you quickly down the path to nowhere and then expect you to be able to figure out how to get back! By then he'll be obliging someone else. When a healthcare start-up faced a safety recall of one of its products, Sure Will dedicated himself to making sure the sales force continued to sell the same product. When a heavy machine company faced an enormous downsizing, he continued to recruit.

As you struggle to get out of the valley, he can take control and lead you and your organization precisely nowhere.

SURE WILL

Will to Self

*I'm a great doer
under stress.*

*The more I take on,
the better for me.*

*If I keep doing
things it will lead
me somewhere.*

Will to Others

*"Leave it to me, I'll
get it done."*

*"Let's work rather
than worry about
results."*

*"Let's assume
responsibility, and
do it."*

Is this you?

*Don't take things on unless you understand
why you should be doing them.*

Positive Strength

Taking responsibility.

Keep Your Change Levers Well Oiled

Your capacity to deal with change includes specific tools you already possess. They make your resolve productive when you are in the valley. They are the things that lift your descent through the valley, like *levers* that help you turn the corner and head toward the better place.

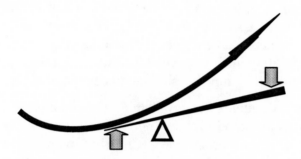

These levers can be any healthy, positive thing you do to take care of your self in difficult times, for example, time alone, hobbies, strong relationships, or meditation.

You need to know what your levers are so you can keep them readily available. We all have different ones. Imagine a sudden loss happening to you in the next few minutes. Who would you call? Where would you go? Who would support you? Where would you start?

Here's the nugget about levers: The leaders who fair poorly when confronted with major change are those who fail to pay attention to these tools when they're *outside* the valley, during the good times. They let their change levers rust.

When your leadership identity is clear and these levers (particularly key relationships) are well oiled, your resolve finds a productive pathway out of the valley. When your levers are stiff and corroded— and your purpose no more than a feeble wish—chances are your resolve will take a long time to find traction and move you upward.

So if you could choose one living person, place, or thing to be available to you whenever you pass into the valley, who, where or what would it be? Now do something immediately about preparing before you get there.

Back to Chris and His Journey Through the Valley

When Chris lost his job and returned home with his severance package in hand, he was in a state of shock, and he knew it. A voice in his head told him not to follow his impulse to run to a lawyer and fight back. He knew from experience that his emotions would be going crazy for a while, and that he needed a distraction. He decided to spend a few days painting his house with his brother, a project he had been putting off for a long time because he'd been too busy.

That time away from his troubles was invaluable. His relationship with his brother was always good for him. It got him thinking about something other than his career predicament. Chris had many pangs of disappointment and confusion along the way, but by sharing them with his brother, he could let them pass by without detriment. When his old colleagues called to wish him well, Chris kept the conversations positive and hopeful.

A couple of weeks later, the house looked a lot brighter and Chris declared himself ready for action. Feeling his newfound resolve, he created in his journal a clear statement about his new emerging leadership identity—his Fish—to serve him on his newfound journey. He wrote about the way he felt a senior executive ought to lead an organization through a major change like the one he'd just experienced. This also reminded him of his core strengths.

"Change like I have seen in the last few weeks is inevitable in this day and age. There will always be pressure to create improvements in business performance, and that leads to lots of takeovers and mergers and, frankly, casualties like me. I know for certain that in any change situation, what I stand for—my Fish—is treating people with dignity above all things. Many executives say this, but when the crunch comes, they fail to put it first. I can—and I always will, especially after the way I was just treated.

"This may be why the new bosses didn't ask me to stick around to help in the merger. It is more important than profits and customers, because to me it's the foundation of success for any enterprise.

"What I mean by dignity is very clear to me. It means treating people as I would wish to be treated in similar circumstances, being realistic, and communicating the truth of the situation (including that there are things they can't be told), and then doing all within my power to help them on their journey. It means taking the time to listen to their views. I'm starting to wonder whether the electronics industry, with its tough business style, is the right place for me."

From this point on, Chris's resolve and new identity grew enormously. He committed himself to finding a new leadership role in an organization where his Fish could "swim." He was swimming in a matter of months.

Sally Built a Doorway to a Brighter Future

Sally's support came from her family, her friends, and her faith. People let her know with certainty that they would support her if she were laid off. After four weeks of agonizing delay, Sally came to a new realization: she couldn't do any worse than the leaders trying to combine her organization with another.

With the support of her family, she decided that before becoming a casualty, she would do her level best to let senior management know what she could achieve. She prepared a plan to deal with the changes the company needed and presented it to her superiors. She was clear and bold in expressing how they could achieve their purpose of cutting costs by a different path. To her surprise, the senior management team listened. Through her courage to build her own doorway to the future, she actually ended up as head of her department, which suffered few layoffs after all.

Sally learned that a loss of identify is a *feeling* and not necessarily a *fact*. And there may be some gold on the other side of the valley.

Get a Clear View Across the Valley

When you decide that your trip through the valley can take you somewhere better, you need to bring that "somewhere" to life in your mind. I call this your commitment to the *Mountains of Hope*. On these mountains stand your leadership identity and your goals —your destination—even when your faith in them is badly shaken. For Chris, the mountains represented his commitment to finding the right place for his Fish to swim. For Sally, it was her belief in the right way to run her department. For Paul and his colleagues at the bank, it was keeping the business going.

The clearer you make the mountains—and the more often you and your team look up and see them—the more likely you are to reach them in a reasonable amount of time. They draw you toward somewhere positive—somewhere with greater opportunity for success in achieving your purpose.

You may call the process "visioning," "goal-setting," "performance improvement," or just plain "figuring out where the hell we're going." I call it creating a greater leadership purpose. The work of creating the Mountains of Hope and the strategies to get there is best done in small groups. The act of sharing—by verbalizing, writing, and working through the new goals of the organization—reduces fuzziness and builds the resolve of the group as a whole. If your trip into the valley is alone, it's great work to do with your Board.

In these times, it's valuable to know that your organization is a collection of people just like you, passing through the valley. Anything that helps you personally build and demonstrate commitment to the Mountains of Hope—like friends, colleagues, meetings, plans, strategies, and missions—is probably going to work for them, too. Your own change strategy can have an exponentially powerful effect upon your team. It's The Rule again: *First, use your own change levers with excellence.*

One important point: The Mountains of Hope are *real goals*, not abstract concepts or feelings. For example, "We need to regain 12 percent market share" versus "We need to boost morale somehow." The top of each mountain must be a clear and tangible destination. Remember, many people have to look at them and use their image to re-create their own leadership identity. Think of them as a magnet drawing you all forward.

Beware the Pit of Doom!

I should point out that the alternative to moving toward the Mountains of Hope can be very unpleasant indeed. When you and your team can't do the work of defining the Mountains of Hope, you can easily become victims of events—defending your territory and waiting in dread for the next blow to strike.

This initiates a downward spiral in which you dwell on the causes of problems rather than their solutions and patch over difficult issues rather than address them.

When this happens, you will inevitably fall into the Pit of Doom.

In the Pit of Doom, any thoughts of the Mountains of Hope are far too late. This part of your leadership journey is about to come to an abrupt halt. It's time to re-create your leadership identity somewhere else. You should spend whatever determination you have in search of a new job. Staying in the Pit to the bitter end is rarely necessary.

Do any of these phrases sound familiar?

> *We're losing all our experienced people and not replacing them.*
>
> *We can't meet a single deadline.*
>
> *The IT infrastructure is falling apart.*
>
> *We can't keep up with all the customer complaints.*
>
> *We may have to delay a pay day.*

They're all symptoms that you may be on the slippery slope to the Pit of Doom. Such a slide occurs when the magnitude and pace of change exceeds the abilities of the leadership team to deal with the change. Simply put, they can't cope with the change. Often, the members of the team jump ship because they see the pit coming before the leaders do.

The cause of the change doesn't matter. I've seen entire organizations attempt to avoid impending doom by doing things that only end up accelerating the fall. If you read the newspapers, you know that occasionally these desperate activities cross legal and ethical boundaries.

That's why you have to keep pulling on your change levers and keep the Mountains of Hope in your sights from the earliest moments when you discover your resolve. A sluggard is the Pit of Doom's best friend.

The enemy of your change capacity is often your own internal chitchat, luring you toward the Pit of Doom and away from the Mountains of Hope. One leader told me, "There have been so many layoffs in our industry, we're all talking about when it will happen to us." It's amazing how much victimization is actually self-generated. Those around us amplify our feelings of victimhood until our fantasy doom becomes reality. When you're stuck in the "waiting for the other shoe to drop" or the "bad things happen in threes" way of thinking, you create artificial barriers to success at a time when there are plenty of real ones to contend with. Don't get sucked in. Start applying The Rule.

Steps Out of the Valley

If you find yourself in the Valley of Despair, here are six things you can do that always help.

1. **Consult Your Board.** Start accepting that the Valley of Despair is just that—a valley. You will get through it. Tell yourself that what you're feeling is perfectly normal and reasonable. Find people on your Board you can trust, and share with them what has happened. Avoid conversations with people who trigger doom and despair.

2. **Seek Out Peace and Quiet.** Create a quiet place where you can find some peace during the day. This is your place for prayer, meditation, or simple physical rest or exercise. Just keep in mind that your inner wounds will heal better if you occasionally take a peaceful rest, calm the chitchat, and quietly reflect on The Mountains of Hope and remind yourself of your Fish.

3. **Write Things Down.** Periods of rapid change are a good time to keep a journal. It helps you keep track and lets you characterize things in your own words. It is a place for you to refine your Fish and record your hopes, fears, gratitude, and plans.

4. **Turn Toward the Mountains of Hope.** Dig out that old mission or vision statement (personal or team) you prepared months ago. Get clear in your own mind what your and your organization's purpose *really* is. Write it down, and start redefining it with your team.

5. **Create Achievements.** Shift your relationship with time toward greater urgency. If you are used to planning quarterly, plan by the month for the next quarter. If you normally plan monthly, now do it weekly. Turn up the urgency dial, and create clear, early, achievable goals. Then communicate these goals just as clearly to your team. Focus everyone on achieving them. Don't let people sit in the Valley of Despair without achievements to be proud of and to celebrate.

6. **Get Involved.** The closer you get to your customer, in the broadest sense, the more nourishment you will derive from seeing

that your purpose is being achieved. This is a great time to lead by example. Your commitment and confidence will be infectious.

Adversity Is Not All Bad

There's a silver lining to all this doom and despair. Adversity has its advantages. One of them is that it draws people toward the Mountains of Hope. Remember how Paul and his people created new ways to run their business after 9/11? Adversity is a time when the resolve of great leaders shines through as they connect themselves and their followers to a common purpose.

There are many books about successful leaders who have demonstrated an amazing ability to focus the hearts, minds, and actions of their followers under terrible adversity. Study them—you might even appoint some of these leaders to your personal Board of Directors. Many of them look back upon their historic leadership moments and modestly conclude that they were at the right place at the right time. This may indeed be true, but something was waiting in them—perhaps some robust change levers to pull on, some immensely powerful Fish, or an innate ability to inspire people toward the Mountains of Hope.

Are similar things waiting in you? For your leader within, expanding your capacity to deal with change is a gift you receive whenever you journey through the Valley of Despair and apply The Rule.

Of course, receiving the gift and appreciating it are quite different things.

Growing Your Change Capacity

Your change capacity grows throughout your leadership journey.

1. *How would others describe your ability to lead through major change?*

2. *Do you seek feedback more or less when you are in the Valley of Despair? What does it say most often?*

3. *Pick a situation when you were in the valley and reflect upon what you learned about your change capacity during that time.*

4. *What are the change situations in which you typically overreact and set off in the wrong direction? Do you have ways to compensate for overreacting to avoid these mistakes in the future?*

Close this exercise by creating a list of your change levers and assess their state of readiness for your next valley. Make a plan to keep them well oiled before you need them.

CHAPTER TWELVE

Let Go of Useless Attachments

Do you ever get the sense that things are not well with your team? Or have you ever walked away from a team meeting with a nagging feeling that something was not quite right, or that your team didn't "get it"? Maybe you've received anonymous feedback that people are unhappy and it makes you feel uncomfortable, or perhaps a member of your Board of Directors has given you some harsh truths you were not expecting. There may even be times when your followers are driving you absolutely nuts!

Those moments of confusion—even pain—in your relationship with your team are *signals*. They're a wake-up call to your leader within. They're telling you that some aspect of your leadership thinking and, therefore, your activity needs adjusting.

Tune In to the Signals

I know from experience that it's easier to avoid these signals until you you're forced to pay attention—or until it's too late. Picture me again in the last few months of my CEO job, madly trying to solve everyone's problems while the signals of my impending demise were staring me in the face. Yes, I got plenty of signals, some of them in direct words from my colleagues, but I was too attached to my way of operating to hear them. I believed that my view of reality and the route to success was unassailable. So I denied the messages. My self-importance pushed my leader within completely out of the picture. Only after I got my marching orders did I see how wrong I'd been not to pay attention to the signals.

There is, however, a reward for recognizing these signals and making a course correction, and it's not just keeping your job: You get to make a valuable adjustment to how you are achieving results.

Has your leader within ever echoed any of the following statements:

> *"I'm really irritated that I've had to ask them for this for the umpteenth time."*

> *"This person doesn't seem to be strong enough to be on my team, but others say he is. I'll go with their view."*

> *"He hasn't done a good job, but he's worked very hard. I'll tell him it's great."*

> *"Personally, I can't stand this person's attitude, but I guess I can't say anything."*

> *"I'll overlook this transgression of the rules, because he's too important to our team's success."*

> *"I know it's my problem, but I'm so busy that I'll just have to duck it for now."*

These are all examples that indicate that the connection between your leader within and your leadership of others has an obstruction. There's something stuck in the way of leading your self according to The Rule.

The most potent signals of an obstruction are self-generated, like the "nagging doubt" that a decision was not right, or the "feeling" that your comments have not been fully understood, or the "hope" that a person will miraculously improve his performance. If you don't get your leader within listening to these signals, you'll never get the obstruction unstuck.

What causes us to miss these signals? One cause is our attitude and habitual way of thinking, which can deafen us to these signals or prevent us from understanding them.

The other is a lack of determination: We simply don't want to face having to press the adjust button. This is particularly true when you are under stress or passing through the Valley of Despair. But remember: Holding on to old baggage leads to a suboptimal leadership style in which your own biases, self-serving opinions and misdirected instincts rule each leadership moment.

Believe me, I know it's easier to ignore these inner signals and crowd them out with urgent business and more pressing thoughts. But that's the pathway to poor performance. Here's what people who ignore signals have said years later.

> *"My obsession with my own needs and strengths left me isolated and constantly disappointed in my team."*

> *"I was too concerned with team harmony. We were so busy being nice to one another that we never achieved our goals."*

> *"I pushed far too hard to keep profits growing. I drove the good people away, produced financial difficulties, and precipitated unethical practices."*

> *"My need to be the sole problem-solver created bottlenecks, made me avoid longer-term issues, and attracted weak people."*

If you resonate with any of these phrases, I can tell you from hard coaching experience that the leaders who said them—some of whom are clients—also said:

> *"I saw the signals, but I failed to pay attention to them early enough."*

Don't let things get to that point for you. Learn to hear the signals and make your adjustments before you go too far off course.

Baggage You Don't Need On Your Journey

Consider these signals as evidence of views you hang onto that you don't need. I call them *expired attachments*. They are the blockages between your leader within and your leader without that you simply don't want. They're outdated methods, styles, opinions—even people—that you hang on to, sometimes to the bitter end, in the mistaken belief that they are helping you achieve your purpose. In fact, they're worse than useless. They stink. When produce expires in the supermarket, you can see or smell the signs immediately. But you can never directly see expired attachments inside the mind of a leader. That's why picking up signals from within and without is so important to you. You need to learn to spot them early and actually *enjoy* letting them go so you're not weighed down by unwanted baggage and odors.

This is a root cause of why many leaders fail. They repeatedly make bad decisions by hanging onto their expired attachments. As these decisions work downstream through their organization, their failure is manifested in their results. It's like putting rotten produce on everyone's shelf. The stench is predictable.

Put the following story about Peter, who has an amalgam of expired attachments, on your stage and look from the balcony. See if you can relate to his experiences. And just to drive my point home, I've highlighted the visible signals and expired attachments as I saw them.

Peter the Not-So-Great

Peter is the head of a small division of a health and beauty conglomerate. During our first meeting, he describes the tremendous growth his division made in its first two years. Unfortunately, he says, the growth has slowed considerably over the past 12 months. He goes on to describe how he built that division from the ground up, finding a factory space, hiring the first five employees, negotiating with suppliers, getting the business rolling, and then growing it tremendously. He describes himself as a "truly committed leader, working 24/7 for the organization."

At one point, there is a polite knock on the door and a man enters. Peter's demeanor changes instantly. Suddenly he is cold, stern, and aloof. Peter is clearly expecting a report, and the man gives a complete and quite positive statement of facts about the manufacturing plant. Throughout, Peter's demeanor never changes; his deadpan stare stays the same.

After the man leaves, Peter's expression returns just as quickly to the same friendliness he showed before. "Don't worry," he tells me, "I'm giving him a hard time for messing up production last month. I'm ignoring him by just communicating the bare minimum, and I know it's driving him crazy. It'll teach him to get it right."

Signal: *Playing emotional games with colleagues.*

Expired Attachment: *To personal power.*

The conversation returns to normal, but a few minutes later, the phone rings. One of Peter's customers is calling to express concern over a shipment of products, three of which failed the customer's quality test. "I'll look into it straightaway," Peter says respectfully before hanging up.

Peter goes through another instant change. His face becomes bright red. He jumps up from his desk and rushes out of his office with me following, down the corridor and across the busy factory floor to the office of the vice president of quality assurance and yells, "What the @#%& have you done to this customer with this stuff?

"I just had the customer on the phone," he continues, still at the top of his lungs, "and you messed up the quality assurance again. Why can't you get the @#%&* tests right? You keep thinking you've got it right, but you don't."

Signal: *Presuming guilt before you even inquire.*

Expired Attachment: *To superiority of own judgment.*

The VP of quality assurance has seen this show before. "Hold on a minute," he says. "Let's have a look." He checks some papers in his files and notes, "Section 3." Peter flies out of the office onto the factory floor and calls a man over—obviously from Section 3. Peter shouts over and over again what the customer said and why it's this poor man's fault. The factory staff stops work to watch.

Signal: *Forcing your view of reality onto people without respect.*

Expired Attachment: *To own view and self-importance.*

Eventually Peter storms back off the factory floor and into his office, and we settle uneasily back into conversation. "As the president of this company, I'm concerned with every customer complaint," he says. "When a customer calls me to complain, I stop what I am doing, I go straight to the shop floor, and I find whoever did it and get things sorted out. The customer is king in my plant. I'm walking the talk."

Signal: Passionately using a catchphrase to support rude behavior to employees.

Expired Attachment: To old dogma.

What's really going on here? Peter has a constant need for the thrill of running a start-up. He loves the feeling of controlling every single element of a business, no matter how small—including the way people feel. After all, it's his baby and he is going to raise it. But it's a teenager now, and he's running it like a toddler. Whenever anything goes wrong, he immediately feels the need to rush in and take control of it like the floor supervisor he used to be.

Signal: Hanging on to a lower-level leadership behavior.

Expired Attachment: To the way I did it as the "right" way.

"Events," Peter says later with regret, "suck me in." In fact, he has such strong personal attachments to the business that it can throw the organization into chaos at a moment's notice. "It's Corporate's fault," he says. "I'm forced to use too many junior staffers who under-perform because of inadequate skills. But what can I do?"

Signal: Placing blame <u>entirely</u> on others.

Expired Attachment: To personal innocence.

Peter explains how the whole business cannot function without him: "I wake up early in the morning, and conduct my own one-man brainstorming session. Some days," he says, "I arrive with five or six good, new marketing or sales ideas to grow the business. I come into the office and send e-mails to people in the organization with all the great ideas—a new compensation scheme to HR; two marketing ideas to Annie, my VP. I energize the whole place when I do this every day."

Signal: Dominating the flow of new ideas without dialogue.

Expired Attachment: To superiority of own ideas.

For a moment, put yourself in the shoes of someone working for Peter. At first, it's very exciting. You experience success and a sense that you're learning from a dynamic master. But all too quickly, the situation deteriorates. You grow frustrated and angry as Peter refuses to give you any creative responsibility. Instead, he dictates to the letter exactly how to do your job. Eventually you feel you have only one decision to make: complain or leave.

Subsequently, the members of Peter's team became dispirited or they resigned. As esprit de corps broke down, so did productivity. Everything spiraled downhill from there. Peter was forced to do more and more because his team did not have the skills and systems needed to perform independently.

When I challenged Peter to recruit a more experienced business leader to take on some of the executive decision-making and grow the business, Peter saw it as a challenge to one of his loyal team members. He snapped back angrily, "Annie is the best head of sales and marketing in the industry. She's never let me down. She's probably distracted by other things these days."

> *Signal: Excusing poor performance in return for loyalty.*

> *Expired Attachment: To dependent person.*

"Annie's always available, even on Saturdays and Sundays when I call my team to make sure problems are solved properly. She's not one of those who grumble about it. She knows that I'm a workaholic, and that I expect her to be working on Sunday, too."

> *Signal: Expecting imbalance in a follower's lifestyle.*

> *Expired Attachment: To inappropriate personal boundaries.*

Four months down the road, Peter was very unhappy. A large conglomerate had bought out his corporation, and he was told that it would combine his division with another. Peter chose to be unhappy and surreptitiously kept fighting to preserve his old way of doing things.

> *Signal: Fighting to preserve an outdated mode of operation.*

> *Expired Attachment: To an old regime.*

When the merger finally arrived, he was made VP of sales and marketing for the expanded division. But from the outset, he avoided meetings and problem-solving with his people. The new president was left essentially to run the business without him. His sales and marketing team were constantly trying to figure out how to proceed. Peter's contribution to the business was nonexistent. He began to pride himself publicly on his ability to avoid responsibility and still stay afloat.

Signal: Avoiding people and problems.

Expired attachment: To playing the victim.

His team and the president eventually confronted him with their view of his situation. Despite his talent, Peter was unable to adapt. He left abruptly to run a start-up—his abilities in that area are, after all, core strengths.

The head of quality assurance and the team from the factory floor gave him a particularly enthusiastic send-off.

So much for that sorry story. Can you imagine the kind of chitchat going on in Peter's mind that sent out all those signals of expired attachments?

Interpreting the Chitchat

Are there times when what you stand for as a leader is so important that you need to get to the heart of things immediately? Times when you know that your vision includes essential, even sacrosanct principles and that you must actively apply them to the situation at hand? Times when what you really stand for is tested? Perhaps your chitchat says things to you like: "I'm tough about these principles, and we must act," "I'm walking my talk," "I'm compulsive about quality and getting things right around here," or "Focusing on these things has never let me down in similar circumstances in the past."

Please note that these statements are *not* examples of Peter's chitchat. They are attachments you usually *should* have.

Peter's chitchat was saying to him: "Why can't they get things right here without me?" and "These people haven't got a clue. They messed up things for me—again" and "I can't get anything done around here without having to do it all myself, just like the old days."

Can you see the difference? Peter wasn't just standing on good principles. He believed that his way was the *only* way. He was so attached that his chitchat drove him to *resent* his staff for thinking differently. This resentment flooded the situation. He quickly lost his compassion and denied that he needed to treat people on his team with dignity. His expired attachments led him far across the boundary of acceptable behavior. Peter's leader within put him on a collision course whenever he came under stress.

Collision Course

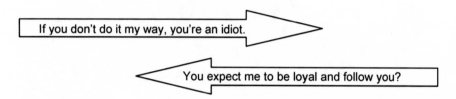

An inner signal of resentment toward people you work with is always an enormous red flag. It's time to stop and call an emergency meeting of your Board of Directors to uncover the real causes of your resentment and anger toward colleagues.

By the way, if *your* chitchat has you calling someone (like your boss) a micromanager because you wish to protect your turf and avoid changing things for the better, then *you're* probably the one with an expired attachment. Like Peter, your unassailable brilliance may be getting in the way.

The Slick Prince

I thought Peter had the worst case of self-generated blockages that I had ever seen. The decline in his business was a direct result of failing to let go of his strong opinions about the way he used to do things. But when I met the Slick Prince I discovered an equally potent Rogue. He has an expired attachment to the idea of *not attaching*. In other words, he holds on to the idea of avoiding responsibility.

SLICK PRINCE

Prince to Self

How good do *I* look
in this situation?

Do I need to do
anything at all?

Don't get caught!

Prince to Others

"Not my problem."

"Our position is
evolving."

"You go ahead, just
keep me informed."

Is this you?

Successful leaders deliver results and
own their problems. How long can
you avoid that reality?

Positive Strength

Astute delegation.

You may know people like him. I call him a Prince because in many organizations his avoidance behavior gets him an undeserved promotion. This is a phenomenon I have never been able to fully understand. I believe, at its heart, it's because he has no track record of any failures. After all, how can you fail if you don't accept accountability? In the eyes of some fearful, Howard Coward executive, he is, therefore, the politically perfect promotion candidate.

The Slick Prince's world is full of none-projects. Things like major programs being talked about but never actually starting. Or extensive activities for which there is no clear accountability. He likes to be on committees, but never as chairman. I watched one Prince become the politically perfect candidate appointed as CEO of a large nonprofit organization. Within 30 days all productive work had stopped in favor of none-projects. I couldn't coach him because he couldn't attach to our definition of purpose (improved results). What an unmitigated disaster.

I hate to say this, but if you're in a large organization and your boss is a Slick Prince, your chances of getting a promotion can be, regrettably, quite good. But make sure your leader within stays focused on outcomes and being accountable as you rise.

Is there some Slick Prince in you sometimes? Do you avoid people and situations that need your involvement? If so you need to own the problem and bring your blockages to light.

Now Bring Your Blockages To Light

In the next exercise, the signals from Peter's story come into play for you to create two lists.

First list: Read the signals below and pick one leader you know who, in your experience, exhibits each one. Write their names down alongside the respective signal.

Plays emotional games with people.

Presumes guilt before even inquiring about a situation.

Forces his or her view of reality onto people without respect.

Passionately uses a catchphrase to support rude behavior.

Hangs on to a lower-level leadership style.

Places blame entirely on others.

Dominates the flow of new ideas without meaningful dialogue.

Excuses poor performance in return for loyalty.

Expects imbalance in a follower's lifestyle.

Fights to preserve an outdated mode of operation.

Second list: Don't beat around the bush. Pick *at least four* of these signals that you know (and that your team would agree) *you* exhibit at times. Write your name alongside those.

Now move on to the exercise box to discover more about expired attachments.

Discover Expired Attachments

For the leaders on your first list:

1. Under what circumstances did you see this signal?

2. Why do you believe they were doing it?

3. What is it they believe about themselves that got in the way?

For the four-plus signals on your second list:

1. Pick a specific occasion when you know you behaved this way. (Example: I was dominating the ideas last week with Jack's team.)

2. What was the chitchat that caused you to act that way? (Example: Frustration at my team.)

3. What did you believe that caused this? (Example: I believed it was easy.)

4. Did that belief turn out to be completely true? (Example: No. It was complicated.)

5. What is your expired attachment in this situation? (Example: My way — the only way.)

6. Replay the circumstance again without the attachment (Example: I would listen more.)

Finish this by picking one expired attachment to discuss with your Board.

Dealing With Blockages

Applying The Rule means facing this hard truth:

> *When you receive a signal that an attachment is preventing you from achieving your purpose, you have to bring it to light.*

Only by bringing it to light, as you did in the previous exercise, can you discover what it takes to let it go and proceed on your journey without it weighing you down. That's how the barnacles get pulled off.

Is your leader within really determined? This is an important question now, because choosing to take action when you hear the signal of an expired attachment is at the heart of leading your self with excellence. Can you see how Peter's inability to see and let go of his attachments eventually brought him down? His determination to start the process of letting go didn't get engaged until it was far too late.

Although these signals may be a whisper, your determination to become a great leader has to speak louder. It should say something like, "That's a signal that *my* attitude needs attention, not everyone else's" or "My journey will be greater if I can learn to let go of this stuff that keeps letting me down."

You might think that letting go of an attachment is as simple as picking one up, looking to see if its value has expired, and then throwing it out. If only it were that easy! The deeper the attachment, the more value we place on it and the harder it is to see and understand, let alone let go. Some things you just care a bit about, and once you see them clearly, or discuss them with your Board, you are motivated to give them up instantly. I remember how quickly I changed my view of the best way to give presentations when I first saw myself

Other attachments are closer to the center of who you are and how you believe the world operates. Leaving behind these deep-seated beliefs, no matter how erroneous, can require a lot of work and support.

Look at Peter. He never came to his senses when his team approached him about the impending disaster his avoidance was creating. His infatuation with his own ideas was intractable. Even when he saw that he was denying the dignity of others, he was unable to change despite genuinely enjoying interacting with people.

I can tell you that job stress causes leaders to hold on far more. That's because when you're anxious, you can get too involved or too detached. One globe-trotting client has a large sign on the back of his office door. It reads H.A.L.T. He told me, "It stands for Hungry, Angry, Lonely or Tired—those are the conditions under which I have to slow down because I get too attached to the animal in me and I end up doing more harm than good. I should add a J for jet-lagged, but it doesn't make a word."

Is the stress of your day forcing you to suppress rather than attend to important inner signals? I recommend to my clients that they apply The Rule and ask this question out loud when they travel home from work each day. It's a private way to surface attachments that are getting in the way of performance.

Relationship Blockages

It's particularly easy to create the attachments to the wrong people in your organization, rather than those who can help you become more successful. For example, it's easy to like people who are like you or loyal to you. The worst manifestations of this can be racism, sexism, ethnocentricity and, lower down the scale, the old-boy network. But even in a milder form it can be dangerous.

One client of mine told the story of how he realized one day, sitting in his executive meeting, that all the people in the room—whom he recruited—were male and dressed just like him. Does that story resonate with you?

In fact, leaders can attach to people who are loyal to them to such an extent that, when there is a natural divergence in their affairs, they find it very difficult to let go and encourage people on their journey elsewhere. Loyal followers can even overattach to the power of the boss to reward and give sustenance. These kinds of attachment cause people to give up their Fish in return for apparent job security. Such organizational devotion is never healthy.

Think about your team for a moment and see if any of these phrases ring true.

"The people loyal to me are often the worst performers."

"There's no diversity in age, sex, and ethnic background."

"There's no steady turnover of people moving up and out."

"I'm uncomfortable when they do work outside my control."

If any of these resonate with you, its time to take a look at the extent of the attachment and see whether you need some adjustment.

Attachments to People

Create a table with 20 important people in your organization whom you interact with.

1. Rate each of them from 1 to 10 according to the quality of the outcomes you <u>expect</u> from them in order to achieve <u>your</u> purpose.

2. Rate them again according to the quality of their <u>actual</u> output in the past few months. Don't bend your standards — listen carefully for signals of expired attachments.

3. Now rate them on the loyalty you feel they have to you in achieving the team's goals.

Analyze the list of ratings and see if you are attached to people who are not helping achieve your organization's purpose.

Are there other individuals, on or off this list, you should acknowledge more?

Press the Adjust Button

You can press the adjust button to get rid of your blockages when you are alone or with your team members or your Board of Directors, or in any other situation. It's a habit that's worth learning. It's not a one-off event. It's any valid technique that helps your leader within avoid hanging on to expired attachments that limit your success. You can do it anytime and even learn, with a little practice, to achieve a state where you are constantly making small adjustments to fit the circumstance. The feeling of mastery it produces is incredibly affirming.

OVER-ATTACHMENT

Leading My Self	Leading Others
Am I properly identifying and letting go of practices and people that don't serve our greater purpose?	Am I encouraging my team to point out outdated views and procedures that inhibit success?

When you use one of the lenses, you are pressing the adjust button. You stop your normal course of thought, put the lens into your line of sight, and get another view of your possible attachments, courtesy of The Rule. Make a regular practice of doing this, especially with your Board. And, of course, when the signals are clear you need to find the determination to make some changes.

Get into the regular habit of pressing the adjust button. Look deliberately at people, situations and timeframes to see if your views are "stuck" and limiting performance. You can do this simply by asking, (1) What outcomes do I expect? (2) What outcomes do I get? (3) What can I learn about my leadership from the difference?, and (4) What will I now do differently?

Can you see how these questions, when asked repeatedly and consistently, provide a steady stream of small blockages to overcome rather than an accumulated pile to conquer?

Trust: The Place to Start

There is one distinct element of your leadership identity that is worth *holding* onto, and that is **trust**—in your self, in your strengths and in others. Unlike inflated or unreasonable expectations (or even perfectly reasonable ones, for that matter) trust offers you a foothold in the future that has some constancy.

When you choose to trust people, you attach them to your hoped-for future leadership success, and that attaches you to theirs. When you lose trust with somebody, you start to remove him or her from your picture.

Trust, of course, is never constant. In any relationship it is a variable that depends on past experience. But *starting* from a position of trust often becomes self-fulfilling. Try it. And don't forget to use the "Game Over" button with compassion and dignity when it needs to be pressed.

Let Go, Commit, and Grow

When a hermit crab begins to outgrow its shell it faces some of the challenges that all leaders do if they are to achieve their true leadership identity.

The crab must leave the safety of the familiar, even though its shell still fits, but is a little confining and limiting. It must be willing to brave the rain, hot sun, and predators in the search for a new home.

This new home must be one that it can grow into—a shell that's a little too big at first and one that allows for some growing room.

While the crab is enduring the weather and lack of protection, it must not be tempted to run back to the old shell, although it could still fit for a while longer. It must turn its back on the old shell of the past forever and run along the beach in search of its new home.

Where are you right now? Are you still in the old shell feeling confined and limited? Are you out on the beach with a positive and determined spirit in your leadership moments? Do you even want a new shell—a leadership identity that really will make a big difference?

Do you have the faith that the self-doubt and wind and rain and sunburn will be worth going through to get your purpose clear and get to your destination?

Will you build a great team to take you there? A team who will find their leadership identity fulfilled through you?

Good. Hold on to that idea and let go of your old shell.

CHAPTER THIRTEEN

Energize a Great Team Performance

A young Russian orchestra conductor, already famous in his own country, was asked to conduct a short series of concerts with an American orchestra. On the first morning of rehearsals, he stood before the orchestra, asked for silence, and spoke to the musicians on his team for the first time.

"Do not concern yourselves with me, my name, or where I come from," he told them. "You may call me Maestro. In the last year I have conducted the greatest orchestras in Russia. Our performances have been heralded as the greatest concerts of all time.

"You will need to perform beyond excellence if you are going to match that performance. I, your Maestro, will take you there. In the next two days, you will work 16 hours a day and I will lead you to perfection."

Just then a voice from the orchestra said, "Hey, whatever your name is, I'm going for coffee!"

Things continued downhill from there.

The right to govern the territory that exists between you and your team is not yours automatically. You have to earn it through real leadership work. Your reputation alone is not sufficient. Before accepting you into the team space, the members look at the way you lead your self—and then they decide if they want to be led by you. And they keep deciding. They have the choice each day to let their leadership journey and yours coincide.

When you take the lead, no matter how, when, and for how long, your team recognizes a special power you hold in your hands. It's the light of your leadership. When you lead yourself with excellence, your light illuminates the path toward the team's greater purpose.

Start asking: What's it like to be on *my* team, feeling *my* light?

1. **The quality of my light:** Do I always operate from a place of integrity, performing to the standards I expect of others, listening with both ears and bringing my whole self to the situation?

2. **The force of my light:** Is my beam too weak to guide people? Or is it so forceful that it blinds people from taking the first step. Or does it shine strongly around *me* but weakly in the far reaches of my team where it's most needed?

3. **The rhythm of my light:** Is it erratic and unpredictable? Does it dart in and out at the wrong time dazzling like a strobe? Or does it have a comforting rhythm—one that shows balance and predictability?

4. **The focus of my light:** Can it be aimed where it's most needed or does it go too high, or low, or in a scattershot beam?

Think seriously about your answers to these questions. Are there any pangs of regret or doubt emerging? These are the signals we talked about in the last chapter. They're the signs of blockages between your leader within and the way you're leading others. Don't let them stay submerged. Bring them into the light. Start sorting them out.

Think again about the Maestro's failure in shining his light. When you stand in front of *your* team, is it about *them* or about *you*?

Here's a more positive story about a team leader's light.

It happened in an English boy's grammar school. The team had been picked—not to play sport, but to put on a play. The school's drama teacher, Mr. Newton, had decided to follow up his successful version of Shakespeare's *Hamlet* with a famous Irish comedy, *The Playboy of the Western World*. Dress rehearsals were just starting when one skinny boy wearing a green dress, makeup, and a wig—the leading lady— came to Mr. Newton as he sat talking to the technicians in front of the stage.

"I'm sorry, sir, I just can't do this," said the 12-year-old, pulling off the wig. "Everyone's poking at me and making fun of me dressed up like this. And the whole school will make fun of me after we do the play. I've thought about it, sir, and I think it's best if you pick someone else to play a woman."

Mr. Newton quietly excused himself from his conversation with the technicians. He led the boy to the seats at the back of the theater where they sat down together. The boy was expecting anger and a string of arguments about letting down the cast at the last minute, but he was determined to avoid embarrassment by quitting.

"There's something you don't know about me and it's important that I explain," said Mr. Newton quietly. "I have an amazing picture in my mind. I can see the complete play as it will be performed by all the boys in the cast, including you. I picked a team capable of delivering a great performance—better than any play we've ever done. I could have picked you to play a man rather than a woman, but I decided you and I could do it. I bet that of all the boys who auditioned, we would have the audience believing you're a powerful Irish woman. My confidence in your achieving that is higher now than when you auditioned.

"I don't see them laughing at you after this play. They'll be congratulating you because you convinced them you were an Irish woman. You can leave the cast if you truly believe you can't do it, but I'm still certain that we both made the right bet. You can trust me on this—and what's more," he joked, "that wig looks stunning on you."

Mr. Newton was right. And that skinny Irish woman with the wig and falsies was me. After each of the three shows, we all received accolades. Some people even came to multiple performances. Any fears I had that my school chums would make fun of me were replaced with pride when I saw they had a deeper respect for the Irish woman within me who had moved them.

Look at the difference between Mr. Newton and the Russian conductor. The Maestro's light was shining on him—not on his team. He never started to create a great team performance. Mr. Newton could see the greater person I could become by playing on his team. (How's *that* for a definition of a great team leader?) For Mr. Newton, it wasn't about him but about me. When he shone his light, he lifted me, heart and soul, toward that future leadership identity he imagined for us all. His confidence and belief in *me* infected me.

Next time you stand in front of your team and shine your light, be certain who you're shining it for. It's about who *they* can become, rather than about you.

Great Team Playing **is** Leading

When you play on a *great* team, like me and Mr. Newton, it's as though your "team player light" shines back in response to the lights from your leader and teammates. Your spirits connect. That kind of connection is the foundation of a truly great team performance that grows people. Large organizations spend millions trying to create it.

What is it that causes this team connection to work superbly in some situations and not so much in others? Hint: Think about The Rule. Yes, it's how *your* leader within governs your team leadership. The worst team playing experiences leave a residue of reasons *not* to give the very best to a team leader. And without the right spirit and determination in the leader, the team commitment to a great performance is never solidified.

Organizations deploy all kinds of teams to get results. But many times it seems as though people are unable or unwilling to shine their team player light. They've been burned by prior experiences and it's dim and unfocused. Although they try to share accountability for achieving the team's purpose—improved outcomes—they can't get any real positive traction.

Young managers ask me repeatedly why anyone would fully commit to lead or play on a team in an organization. Cynically, they say that if you're smart (like the leaders we read so much about) you won't fully commit to any team. You should just *act* committed. They ask: How can you be a member of a team, sharing your talent, in a climate where solo performances are revered and rewarded, and where the leader's primary concern seems to be whether the team performance makes him or her look good?

The answer is this:

> ***Your leader within must believe that team leading and team playing are <u>virtues</u>—desirable core strengths worth deploying and developing.***

You have to know at a deeper level that this is how great things happen for you and your group. Whether this comes from your early experiences, like me and Mr. Newton, or from later ones in your working life, you have to act in the belief that committing fully offers an experience that far exceeds the most heroic individual performance. Only when your leader within is certain of this can you expect your team to follow suit.

And if you blame the absence of that belief on your organization— "Nobody respects team playing here" or "My boss doesn't even understand what my team does"—you are missing the point completely. You *are* the organization.

Think about your own team for a moment and use this lens.

TEAM PLAYING

Leading My Self

Am I committed to the belief that both great team leading <u>and</u> team playing are vital strengths?

Leading Others

Do I demonstrate my commitment to great team playing through my own behaviors and the way I support others?

The nugget here for your leader within is this:

> *You need to have a great <u>team player</u> performance as a central element in the identity you want to create for yourself as a leader.*

All team-leading situations offer you the opportunity to be a great team player. You must seize those that use your strengths. It's The Rule again: *To lead team players to a successful performance, you must first lead the team player in you with excellence.* Don't be ambivalent about this one. Showing how you team-play is key to your team leader competence. It's one of the reasons people will commit to belonging to your team.

Get the Feel for Commitment

Like you, your team members have a choice as to where they shine their light, so you will see and feel them making these choices constantly. You are a central part of their decision to commit and remain committed. In fact, over time, you can feel team members constantly being pulled and pushed along the connected-disconnected continuum by their inner and outer forces. This is particularly true with cross-functional teams where the forces pulling people away easily overpower the glue that holds them together.

What's happening is that their chitchat is at work interpreting events and telling them whether they can be safe and successful on your, and anyone else's, team. I call it their *belonging zone*. Since team members are constantly resetting their level of commitment, particularly on cross-functional teams, that belonging zone must have your regular attention.

There's a belonging zone in *your* mind, too. It applies whenever you think of each player on your team and even the team as a whole. There, your leader within is deciding whether people can fulfill, and continue fulfilling, their function on the team. This is never a black-and-white picture. Your team connections are always in motion. Hopefully, for most of your team, it's over toward the "nicely committed" end of the scale. If not, start thinking about how to press the adjust button.

Don't assume that these two belonging zones—yours and your team's—are the same. For example, loyalty to you in a previous job does not guarantee loyalty on your current team. Instead, determine each individual's level of commitment based on track record, personal work ethics, quality standards and, particularly, core attitude toward their and the team's purpose.

I'm sure you know firsthand that the initial period of belonging is very sensitive. People who leave teams later often point back to it as the cause for their departure. This is a well-known problem and many models, instruments, and techniques have been developed to help teams deal with it. Use them but remember that their effect is often short-lived. People never stay in a fixed position in their belonging zone, particularly when the makeup of the team changes frequently. Why? Because they are all on their own unique leadership journey.

Build a Team of Leaders

When you picture your team and their belonging zones, do you see a well-organized, cooperative group of people, or do you see a wide range of personalities, attitudes, and performances? Do you see any rough edges that stick out and cause sparks to fly occasionally? Team playing can definitely bring out the worst in people.

The definition of a *great* team player is not simply someone who is trusted and who works cooperatively with fellow team members. These issues are mostly secondary. What defines a *great* team player starts with the achievement of *their* purpose: the part they need to perform on the team.

Think about it. What is a team player's purpose? It is to improve outcomes for the organization, for their followers (if they too have a team), for those individuals who depend upon them (like their teammates), and for themselves?

Does that sound familiar? It should. It's our definition of the purpose of leadership. Team players have to realize that achieving the team's goals depends on each player creating an excellent leadership outcome for his or her part. In short, they will perform far better when they see themselves as part of a ***team of leaders***.

When this concept takes root in a team, the issues of what people need and how to work cooperatively fall into their rightful place—*behind* achievement of the team's real purpose. Delivering results becomes the first yardstick by which belonging and achievement are measured.

I want you to know with complete certainty that you can trust this concept. When your team feels like it is facing disaster, or the mood meter is heading for "doom," or people are at the lowest end of their belonging zones, return to your (and, by extension, each team member's) leadership purpose. Even when people say they misunderstand you, disagree with you, or simply dislike you as the team leader, return to your purpose—and how you are intending to achieve it. Conflict problems are nothing more than *symptoms*. And shining your leadership light on symptoms without first considering your purpose gives you multiple headaches—it wastes effort and generates false goals.

Diane and Her Global Team

Diane had a blind spot. She avoided symptoms and her team stopped belonging.

She was a senior VP leading a worldwide team of technicians developing next-generation agricultural products for her company. A few members of her team looked to her as their permanent manager, while most others reported to her indirectly via other geographical and functional groups. Like many organizations, the company employed a well-organized system to establish and communicate team goals, strategies, tactics, and milestones as well as organizing team meetings through videoconferencing and webcasts. It was an impressive system that enabled communication on a global scale.

Diane's relationship with her team was at a critical stage. One team member had written a letter of complaint to the CEO and others were skipping her meetings. They were constantly pointing a finger at each other. What was far more important was that they were about to miss a critical milestone on the product-development path.

"I didn't pick most of them in the first place, and I never would have," Diane complained. "They don't have the right skills, they don't cooperate, and many of them don't seem to want to use the project system properly. Most of them are more interested in doing the day-to-day work back in their own organization rather than our team's work, and they're constantly bickering or complaining that they don't have a sufficient budget." She followed this with a detailed criticism of each of her team members.

It was a large team, working on a complex project, so members were experiencing numerous conflicting forces in their belonging zones.

Diane was in trouble. This project could be a career-changing event for her. When the previous manager left, Diane was chosen not because of her experience, but because her boss was willing to make her available quickly. She felt that her team members knew more than she did and that she could never catch up.

Once Diane understood the concept of belonging zones, her view of her team expanded. Using The Rule, she began to examine how well she was enabling the support they needed from across the entire company. At the time she said, "I'd always assumed that I couldn't do anything about their commitment because they are not under my direct management."

She pressed the adjust button this way: At the beginning of the next videoconference meeting, she broke the rigid agenda set by the project management system and said, "Please, could we go one by one around the team and say what the three most important issues are on our plate."

Picture each person describing the three most urgent problems he or she had to tackle for the project to succeed. Diane waited patiently for everyone to speak. She was doing balcony work and sensing each person's level of belonging. By the time they finished, they had all caught up with the sad and confused state of the project. Diane could see all the issues facing her team very clearly.

She then looked at the published agenda for the meeting and asked three questions that changed the direction of her team for good:

1. "Why are so many of those important issues not on our meeting agenda for today?"

2. "Can we put them on the agenda and try to resolve them together before we finish the meeting?"

3. "What more can we do <u>together</u> to get all the issues onto our plate, so we can see them, resolve them, and get the project back on track?"

She had used The Rule to engage each member's leader within to move further into the belonging zone. (Try this with your team)

For Diane, it was just the start of pressing the adjust button with her team. After the meeting, she took time to listen to individual issues and prepare for the inevitably difficult discussions with her boss. She chose not to see people as failing or threatening her. This made her more open to solving every aspect of their problems, including their issues with her leadership.

Here's the nugget that Diane learned about relationships with a team of leaders: When you shine your light upon your team members in any leadership moment, you have a choice to make about the people in front of you. It impacts how you relate together as you go about solving problems and making decisions.

When you choose to see your team as leaders on their own journey *developing* into the greater leader you (at some level) know they can become, you make *them* the focal point of success. You become the *enabler* of their performance and they start to belong a whole lot more.

But if your leader within can't picture people this way, you will never create the kind of connections and belonging that create a great team performance. That, among others, was the Maestro's problem. It was Diane's too, but with The Rule she overcame it permanently.

Think about it. What kind of boss gets the best performance out of you? One that simply wants you to deliver so that his or her goals are met, or one that encourages and helps you to grow as far as you can in delivering results?

Now, for a moment, focus on each member of your current team. Imagine each person's face in turn looking at you from the other side of the lens as you ask the questions.

```
             TEAM OF LEADERS

   Leading My Self          Leading Others

  Do I acknowledge this    Am I actively supporting
   member as a leader      this member and building
  furthering his or her     his or her belief in an
  journey through a great   exceptional performance?
       performance?
```

As you process the insights that emerge from this lens you'll feel the adjust button being pressed on your relationships. Try not to exclude any of your team members. If you do, ask yourself if skipping is a signal of an expired attachment.

Energize the Team Space

What's in the *team space* between team players that the Maestro invaded and Diane ignored?

Picture a nuclear reactor in which uranium atoms bombard one another with neutrons and split. A moderating substance between the atoms controls these potentially explosive chain reactions. Your leadership powers—the moderating substance—works *between* leaders (that is, team members) to help them understand how to achieve their individual purpose within the context of the team's greater purpose.

Too much moderation, and the team may never achieve its purpose. Too little, and the team could explode in a blinding flash of wasted effort, ill feeling, and disarray. Just the right amount and great things can be achieved with all the energy.

It's this space between the players that's clearly your domain. When you operate from that perspective, the issue of enabling a great team performance becomes much clearer. Spending too much time and effort doing the work of your team members and too little doing your own work of leading the team space can be the pathway to the Pit of Doom for you all. (Remember Micromanager Mary?)

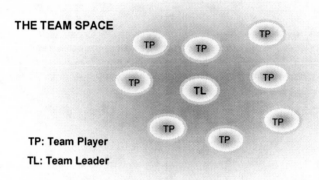

THE TEAM SPACE

TP: Team Player
TL: Team Leader

Picture this team space containing things your team members share and need in order to succeed. Things like their shared feelings (morale), understanding of purpose, how far they've come, how they must proceed together, and who they can depend on for help. If you could project this team space onto an enormous screen, you would see a picture constantly in motion, with some parts clear and others murky; some parts in black and white and others in bright color; some team members causing collisions and others weak and needing your support.

By far the most valuable contribution you make to the team space is leading your self with excellence. When you operate on a balanced platform, articulate your purpose clearly and deploy the right attitude and impact, your team of leaders can see how to lead themselves with excellence.

In addition, there are some essential skills to learn that are disproportionately valuable in energizing the entire team space:

1. **Purpose Building:** This work establishes, and constantly reshapes, the team's focus on the outcomes expected of

them so that the team stays synchronized despite the forces trying to knock you all off balance. This is the most important practice for you to master.

2. **Setting Ground Rules:** These are the basic operating principles and structures governing how people should work comfortably together day to day and remain as productive as possible—even when they are far apart organizationally, geographically, and ideologically.

3. **Reinforcing Team Tenets:** Those shared expressions of what the team stands for, like "All for one..." and "Our credo is...," that are the instant rallying cries that unify the team toward its highest purpose, particularly when you are not present.

4. **Opening Release Valves:** These are the mechanisms you put in place that diffuse the inevitable and highly destructive emotional tensions that arise and build among people working closely together, like one-on-one meetings and team attitude checks.

5. **Running Great Meetings:** The objective of your meetings is for your team members to catch up, solve problems, make decisions, stay synchronized, and gear up for what is ahead.

These are tools by which you can make the team space a great place in which to live, perform, and succeed. But before we move on to talk more about No. 1, Purpose Building, let me remind you again that these pale in importance to bringing The Rule into play on every occasion.

The Gift of Clear Purpose

Most people can be successful leaders in familiar and favorable situations. But in the real world, you will face numerous times when you don't know what to do, where to get answers, or how to make yourself understood.

Even if you have a reputation as an inspiring and visionary leader, you will never achieve your leadership purpose—never—without your leader within understanding that the forces of change constantly try to destroy whatever shared clarity of purpose your team has already achieved. And only you, with your complete view of the team space, can know when and how to rebuild that shared sense of clarity when it is damaged.

Here's the big nugget about building and rebuilding a clear purpose for your team:

> *The best vision (goals, strategies, tactics, milestones, measures, metrics, and dashboards) for your team is one that <u>anticipates</u> that forces will always destroy clarity.*

You lead your self with excellence when you anticipate the forces that destroy clarity in people's minds, including your own. When you do that you make purpose building, or rather purpose rebuilding, a central part of your strategy to keep the team space energized.

Ask yourself now: How much time do I spend doing these activities?

> *Updating goals, plans, and tactics.*

> *Creating <u>simple</u>, <u>adaptable</u> pictures and plans to guide people as conditions change.*

> *Anticipating rather than solving problems.*

> *Resetting expectations at the outset of leadership moments.*

> *Spending time listening to changing circumstances versus talking about them.*

> *Responding quickly when people lose their sense of belonging.*

> *Recruiting people that are masters at solving new problems rather than old.*

These are practical examples of anticipating issues and maintaining clarity of purpose for you and your team. They all keep the team space constantly energized toward achieving your purpose. They are exclusively your responsibility as the leader of the team space.

Now think again about your team but this time put your *whole* team back under the lens:

The journey ahead for you and your team will be full of complex problems, challenging goals, and strained relationships. You will indeed be lucky if that's not the case. Creating the great team performance you want requires you to fully enable *others* to achieve results far beyond their own expectations.

Can you accept your responsibility for the team space and support each of your team members on their leadership journeys? Can you shine your light so that the journey is about them and not about you? Can you do all you can to give the gift of clear purpose when the forces of change seek to make things murky?

If you've come this far, I know you can.

CHAPTER FOURTEEN

It All Comes Down to This

It's a common fallacy to define your leadership solely by what you accomplish. Especially when you live in a world that places more value on what you've got, where you've been, and what you've done than it does on who you are and the leader you're trying to become.

Leadership is a serious business. What matters first and foremost is who you are—in your innermost self, where your leader within resides. Your past, present, and future achievements are no more or less than the outward expression of how your leader within operates. It's your leader within that does the developing. It's your team that responds with a greater performance.

> *You will not become a great leader by doing more but by your leader within discovering more of who you are through what you're doing.*

Do you get this point? It's fundamental yet so easily overlooked. If you want to make great strides as a leader, you have to choose to discover more about yourself. It's those discoveries on your inner landscape that lead to greater achievement in the outer world of your team. And when you can do the discovering *as you're leading,* the pace of achievement can really get going.

But there's an important line in the sand to be crossed. Your coach can't, and shouldn't, help you cross it. You have to place the responsibility for your future success squarely on your own shoulders. Only then will you find the deep conviction and satisfaction that comes from knowing that it's *your* leadership journey to create *your* leadership identity in the world. Happiness is an output of your journey, not an input. The choice to make a big difference is yours, and yours alone, to make. After all, if *you're* not determined to learn for your own good, why would anyone else want to invest in you?

As one CEO says: "Keeping myself in top form and growing is the most serious leadership work I do. It touches everyone in the entire organization. It's also the toughest and most satisfying."

This book has been all about helping you discover how to do that satisfying "serious leadership work." When you read this book you're doing it. When you choose to equip your journey with a great Board of Directors, or focus on playing from your core strengths, or work to give clarity to your amazing leadership identity, you're doing it. In the depths of the Valley of Despair or on the peaks of the Mountains of Hope, when you consciously choose to deploy the right attitude and create a great leadership impact, you're doing it. And of course when you let go of your outdated attachments and shine your light to help your team of leaders achieve amazing results, you're doing it. It's all the work of The First Rule of Leadership: *To lead others to success, you must first lead your self with excellence.* That's one last time. Let it guide you in every leadership moment.

I know from years of coaching that it's so easy to fall back into the old way of thinking that it's "them" not "me" that has to do the work and grow. It leads you to the erroneous belief that leadership development is done for you—or to you—by someone who wants more out of you. You now know that's not true. It's also "serious leadership work" to avoid letting yourself slip back into that all-too-comfortable way of thinking.

It's my ardent hope that in these pages, your leader within has discovered more of who you are as a leader through applying The First Rule. If you've taken the courageous step of translating your discoveries into action, you are already on a journey of greater achievement. When you learn to apply The Rule in all your leadership moments, you will discover how *everything* starts getting better— results, relationships, and especially your self-confidence. You open the door to a journey of not only far greater but also far happier achievement. Don't let finishing this book dampen your resolve.

I would like to close with this quote from a CEO I have coached for some years:

"There are many leadership moments these days when I know for certain that I am giving the very best of who I can be as a leader. It's strange, because I always imagined that there would be a rush of exhilaration in a moment of mastery. There isn't. But there is a joyful feeling of being in a place where I am completely unstressed, comfortable, trusted, and confidently bringing all I am to the situation at hand. The only phrase I can think of to describe it is that it's like coming home."

Now you, take The Rule and go on...and welcome home.

COMPLETE
GALLERY
OF
ROGUES

HOWARD COWARD

TOLERANT TESSA

ANGRY BASTARD

CHARMER CHARLIE

FAST-TRACK LIZ

CARING CARLA

DARTH VADER

FEARLESS FRED

JUDGE MENTAL

SLICK PRINCE

FUZZY HEAD

DANGEROUS DAN

MICROMANAGER MARY

SURE WILL

SWEETIE PIE

Acknowledgments

To the clients of Leadership Strategies—the real creators of this work— I owe an enormous debt of gratitude. It has been in helping you achieve success that First Rule of Leadership has been forged into a powerful tool. It should be no surprise that you find aspects of yourself in the concepts, examples, and caricatures in these pages. Thank you from the bottom of my heart. When you share your day-to-day leadership moments, the journey of your coach is enriched enormously.

Many clients and other leaders have graciously given their time to review manuscripts, test approaches, and even conduct a "blind" test of the voice of the book. My thanks to you all and especially to the specific contributions of Mark Alexander, Alfred Altomari, David Colatriano, Bruce Collings, Bill Cordivari, Sharon D'Agostino, Alan Dowie, David Eastin, Greg Evans, Marcus Healey, Paul Jellinek, Connie Kallback, James F. Kerwin, Jon Last, Richard Linderman, Robert Linkin, Michael McNamara, Greg Mario, Paul Mignon, Alan Morgan, Colin Morgan, Jay Morris, Jeffrey Nugent, Mike Paul, Willie Printie, Laura Ross, Josita Todd, Derek Wilson, Jan Marie Zwiren, and Colleen Yates.

Special thanks to Paul Friend of Federal Home Loan Bank of New York for permission to reprint his 9/11 story at the beginning of chapter 8.

I am especially indebted to colleagues at Leadership Strategies who have helped with specific written and verbal contributions to the Total Leadership concepts, and to shaping and editing drafts. In particular I must recognize the major creative contributions of Jerry Lanning, Gary Stine, Rebecca Trobe, and Jim Walters. My thanks also to Ravi Arapurakal, Kathy Bernét, Dana Hilmer, Karen Kushner, Martyn Lee and Meryl Moritz for their reviews and discussions of particular concepts or sections, and to Mary Beth Dittrich for logistical support.

The support and excellent work of my principal editors—Mark Ganem, Rebecca Trobe, and Dana Hilmer—have been truly remarkable. They all possess this amazing magic that turns my "Brummie" English into readable form.

I must also add special thanks to Perry Howze for the incredible Rogue caricatures, to Lisa Marien for her super cover design, to Judy Pilone for her thorough copy editing, and to Jan Marie Zwiren for using her great creative talent in discovering the book title.

And last, and far from least, to my wife, Amy, and to our sons William and Richard. Their support on the decade-long journey of Leadership Strategies has been my strength. How can I ever thank you enough.

Dr. Stephen G. Payne

Stephen Payne is an ex-CEO on a mission. He wants every executive to be the very best leader they can be in every moment of their leadership journey. As the president and founder of Leadership Strategies, Stephen has been coaching CEO's and high-level executives for almost 10 years. He has coached thousands of executives throughout the world, including such clients as: Johnson & Johnson, General Motors, Revlon, AOL Time Warner and Abbott Laboratories.

Stephen has a comprehensive yet straightforward and readily doable approach to performance acceleration called "Total Leadership." It connects the leadership performance you want in the outer world to the powerful workings of your inner landscape. He asserts that you already have all you need to be far more successful, and that you will see a transformative change when you take full responsibility for leading yourself with excellence by unlocking your enormous spiritual and mental potential. Whether coaching CEOs, speaking to groups, or reaching leaders through his book, audio CDs and web site, Stephen coaches leaders to greater clarity, confidence and achievement while sparking deep motivational forces that illuminate new pathways to leadership success.

You can reach Stephen at:

Leadership Strategies

www.LeaderX.com

Coach@LeaderX.com

(800) LeaderX or (800) 532-3379

Printed in the United States
88636LV00004B/415-453/A